Why It's OK
Not to Think for Yourself

We tend to applaud those who think for themselves: the ever-curious student, for example, or the grownup who does their own research. Even as we're applauding, however, we ourselves often *don't* think for ourselves. This book argues that's completely OK.

In fact, it's often best just to take other folks' word for it, allowing them to do the hard work of gathering and evaluating the relevant evidence. In making this argument, philosopher Jonathan Matheson shows how 'expert testimony' and 'the wisdom of crowds' are tested and provides convincing ideas that make it rational to believe something simply because other people believe it. Matheson then takes on philosophy's best arguments against his thesis, including the idea that non-self-thinkers are free-riding on the work of others, Socrates' claim that 'the unexamined life isn't worth living,' and that outsourcing your intellectual labor makes you vulnerable to errors and manipulation. Matheson shows how these claims and others ultimately fail — and that when it comes to thinking, we often need not be sheepish about being sheep.

Jonathan Matheson is Professor of Philosophy at the University of North Florida. His research interests are in epistemology, with a focus on issues concerning disagreement and epistemic autonomy. He has authored *The Epistemic Significance of Disagreement* (2015) and co-edited *The Ethics of Belief: Individual and Social* (2014) with Rico Vitz and *Epistemic Autonomy* (2021) with Kirk Lougheed.

Why It's OK: The Ethics and Aesthetics of How We Live

ABOUT THE SERIES:

Philosophers often build cogent arguments for unpopular positions. Recent examples include cases against marriage and pregnancy, for treating animals as our equals, and dismissing some popular art as aesthetically inferior. What philosophers have done less often is to offer compelling arguments for widespread and established human behavior, like getting married, having children, eating animals, and going to the movies. But if one role for philosophy is to help us reflect on our lives and build sound justifications for our beliefs and actions, it seems odd that philosophers would neglect arguments for the lifestyles most people—including many philosophers—actually lead. Unfortunately, philosophers' inattention to normalcy has meant that the ways of life that define our modern societies have gone largely without defense, even as whole literatures have emerged to condemn them.

Why It's OK: The Ethics and Aesthetics of How We Live seeks to remedy that. It's a series of books that provides accessible, sound, and often new and creative arguments for widespread ethical and aesthetic values. Made up of short volumes that assume no previous knowledge of philosophy from the reader, the series recognizes that philosophy is just as important for understanding what we already believe as it is for criticizing the status quo. The series isn't meant to make us complacent about what we value; rather, it helps and challenges us to think more deeply about the values that give our daily lives meaning.

Titles in Series:

Why It's OK to Be a Slacker
Alison Suen

Why It's OK to Eat Meat
Dan C. Shahar

Why It's OK to Love Bad Movies
Matthew Strohl

Why It's OK to Not Be Monogamous
Justin L. Clardy

Why It's OK to Trust Science
Keith M. Parsons

Why It's OK to Be a Sports Fan
Alfred Archer and Jake Wojtowicz

Why It's OK Not to Think for Yourself
Jonathan Matheson

Why It's OK to Own a Gun
Ryan W. Davis

Selected Forthcoming Titles:

Why It's OK to Mind Your Own Business
Justin Tosi and Brandon Warmke

Why It's OK to Be Fat
Rekha Nath

Why It's OK to Be a Socialist
Christine Sypnowich

Why It's OK to Be a Moral Failure
Robert B. Talisse

For further information about this series, please visit: www.routledge.com/Why-Its-OK/book-series/WIOK

JONATHAN MATHESON

Why It's OK
Not to Think for
Yourself

Routledge
Taylor & Francis Group

NEW YORK AND LONDON

Designed cover image: © Andy Goodman

First published 2024
by Routledge
605 Third Avenue, New York, NY 10158

and by Routledge
4 Park Square, Milton Park, Abingdon, Oxon, OX14 4RN

Routledge is an imprint of the Taylor & Francis Group, an informa business

ISBN: 978-1-032-43826-9 (hbk)
ISBN: 978-1-032-43825-2 (pbk)
ISBN: 978-1-003-36900-4 (ebk)

DOI: 10.4324/9781003369004

Typeset in Joanna and Din
by SPi Technologies India Pvt Ltd (Straive)

Contents

The theme of this book is that you are often better off relying on others. The process of preparing this book certainly went better due to a great deal of help that I received from others.

This book has benefitted greatly from comments from and conversations with the following individuals: Nathan Ballantyne, Heather Battaly, James Beebe, Rodrigo Borges, Gabriele Contessa, Brett Coppenger, Aaron Creller, Everett Fulmer, Shane George, Sandy Goldberg, Adam Green, Thomas Grundmann, Michael Hannon, Julie Ingersoll, Casey Johnson, Valerie Joly Chock, Jason Kawall, Bert Koegler, Justin McBrayer, Ben McCraw, Sarah Mattice, Thi Nguyen, Ted Poston, Parker Settecase, Josh Smith, Alessandra Tanesini, Mike Veber, Sarah Vincent, Jamie Watson, Dennis Whitcomb, and Sarah Wright. In addition, I am thankful for the detailed feedback from two anonymous reviewers. The book is better as a result of their feedback.

Furthermore, I am grateful to audiences at the Eastern Division of the American Philosophical Association, the Northwestern/Notre Dame Graduate Epistemology Conference, the Southeastern Epistemology Conference, the Philosophy of Epistemic Autonomy Conference, the PERITIA: The Ethics of Trust and Expertise Conference, the Bled Philosophy Conference, Northwestern University, Florida State University, and the University of North Florida where portions of this book were presented.

Special thanks to James Beebe who encouraged me to pursue this as a book project, as well as for partnering with me on the grant that funded this research. Thanks also to the John Templeton Foundation for their generous support. This publication was made possible through the support of a grant from the John Templeton Foundation (ID# 61802). Of course, the opinions expressed in this publication are those of the author and do not necessarily reflect the views of the John Templeton Foundation. In addition, a very special thanks to Andy Beck and his team at Routledge for their guidance and support throughout this project.

Finally, I would like to thank my family for their support throughout this project. In particular, I would like to thank my wife, Lesley, and my daughter, Karis, who were both gracious enough to read through this book and encourage me along the way.

"Dare to know! Have courage to use your own understanding."
This, Immanuel Kant (1991/1784) declared, is the motto of
the Enlightenment. Kant saw the inability to use your own
understanding without the aid of another as an unacceptable kind of intellectual immaturity. This sentiment has been
widely shared. For instance, René Descartes (1985/1628: 13)
forbid inquiring minds from relying on the ideas of others,
and John Locke (1975/1689: 23) claimed that even the true
opinions of others failed to result in our knowledge.

The call to think for yourself remains prevalent today. A couple of years ago, a number of scholars from Harvard, Princeton,
and Yale penned an open letter to incoming students.[1] This letter had one central piece of advice: think for yourselves. The
letter writers warned of the dangers of conformity, groupthink,
and 'the tyranny of public opinion.' Those who love the truth
and desire to learn, they argued, needed to think for themselves. These scholars saw thinking for yourself as central to
anyone's education.

The idea that thinking for yourself is central to education
is widely shared.[2] Many see the goal of education to be the
development of life-long learners, or to equip individuals for
a life of inquiry. As a philosophy teacher, I take one of my
central tasks to be getting students to think for themselves
about a number of complex philosophical questions. Further,

DOI: 10.4324/9781003369004-1

I don't think I am an outlier here. For instance, many introductory philosophy texts cite getting students to think for themselves as one of their primary goals.[3]

The value and importance of thinking for yourself is so widespread that, perhaps somewhat ironically, it has gone pretty much unchallenged. In some sense, this book takes up that challenge. Throughout the book, I will be making the case that it is perfectly OK *not* to think for yourself. Thinking for yourself, I'll argue, is overrated, we've held it in higher esteem than we should, and it's time to take it down a notch or two. I take it that this idea will strike you as counterintuitive, to say the least. The counterintuitiveness of this claim just goes to show how widely shared the value of thinking for yourself is, as well as how strongly we value it.

So, the conclusion of this book will strike some as absurd. Like many philosophical claims, what strikes some as absurd strikes others as utterly obvious. The same is likely true here. After all, if we are honest with ourselves, we should realize that we don't think for ourselves all that often. For instance, have you ever taken a deep dive into all of the data on climate change? Have you ever examined the extensive evidence for the effectiveness of flossing on dental health? Have you ever read up on the reasons that caffeine increases alertness? My guess is that while you believe all of these things, you have not done your own research, and I'm here to say that's OK. Even if *you* have done so, it seems clear that most people haven't thought for themselves about these issues, and many more. In general, people *don't* think for themselves about a lot of issues. But, that's OK, or at least that is what I'm going to argue throughout this book. In so doing, perhaps this book will restore some harmony. Since we highly value thinking for yourself, while we don't do it all that often, it would be nice if there was a way to ease this tension within ourselves. I'm going to argue that there is. In this sense, this book will be a kind of defense of our common practices, and in particular, our practice of not thinking for ourselves.

Admittedly, there is an uphill battle to this conclusion. If you find the conclusion counterintuitive, I have my work cut out for me. Of course, I think it would be OK if you just wanted to take my word for it, but since you have this book, I'm assuming you'd like to think for yourself about the issue. I want to make it clear from the outset that I think that's OK too! In fact, I think it's great. As we will see along the way, there is a lot to be said in favor of thinking for yourself. This book is not an indictment on thinking for yourself, it simply argues for a pass for not doing so. It is denying that we are required to think for ourselves. If you're inclined to see the conclusion as obvious, I still think it is worth sticking around. You'll likely see challenges to the conclusion that you hadn't considered, and if nothing else, the journey to the conclusion gets to touch on a number of great issues in epistemology.

KEEPING YOUR HOUSE IN ORDER

Let's start with an analogy. Let me tell you about Rico. Rico is a homeowner. He has an immaculate house, yard, and pool. Guests are always in awe of how well-kept his house is. However, while his house is in order, Rico does next to none of the upkeep himself. He employs housekeepers to clean the house, handymen to handle repairs, yard-workers to keep the landscaping beautiful, and he has pool people to make sure that the pool is well-maintained. Rico might change a lightbulb here or there, but almost all of the upkeep is left to the work of others. While Rico relies quite heavily on others, there is no questioning that his house is in order.

In contrast, let me tell you about Rhonda. Rhonda too is a homeowner whose house is also well-kept. However, unlike Rico, Rhonda does almost all of the upkeep herself. She cleans her own house, does her own yardwork, handles all the repairs herself, and so forth. Rhonda takes pride in her self-reliance and the fact that she does her job well.

Rico and Rhonda have very different house maintenance philosophies. Rhonda has embraced the do-it-yourself (DIY) model, while Rico is happy to outsource and let others do the work for him. Rhonda's method takes more of her time, but it is far less expensive than Rico's. While there are a number of differences between these two competing philosophies, both Rico and Rhonda have houses that are in order. In short, there is nothing defective about Rico's way of maintaining his house. In other words, you don't have to be like Rhonda to have your house in order.

Just as one's physical house can be in order while relying heavily on others, I want to argue that your *intellectual* house too can be in order even while you rely heavily on others. Our intellectual projects, like our house projects, can be undertaken by ourselves or they can be outsourced to others. While there are advantages and disadvantages to each course of action, the central conclusion of this book is that it is OK to outsource a great deal of your intellectual projects. It is OK not to think for yourself. In outsourcing your intellectual projects, you can keep your intellectual house in order. You don't have to do it all yourself.

WHAT IS THINKING FOR YOURSELF?

Before turning to the arguments, we need to get clear on what it even means to think for yourself. Let's start with what it is not. Thinking for yourself is not simply using your own cognitive faculties. It is probably impossible to believe anything without using your cognitive faculties in at least *some* regard. The act of believing itself requires some sort of mental work. After all, you have to be doing the believing! So, this sense of 'thinking for yourself' isn't very interesting – it is inevitable. Any interesting sense of 'thinking for yourself' must require more than simply using your brain in some capacity. A more promising proposal focuses on how you came to have your beliefs, or how you conducted your intellectual projects. When you think for yourself, you conduct inquiry in a particular way.

To fill this out, let's first think about inquiry more generally. What is inquiry? Inquiry is perhaps our central intellectual project. It all starts with a question. Inquiry is a goal-directed activity where we set out to find the answer to a question that we have. So, the aim of inquiry is to settle our question, to uncover the answer to it. In inquiry we are after the truth. When your beliefs are true, you can navigate the world well. As Socrates notes in the *Meno*, if you have a true belief about which road takes you to Larissa, then you will be able to get to Larissa. So long as you are correct about which road it is, you will get there, and you can even guide others there as well. However, we don't want to merely stumble upon the answer to our question, we want to have *good reasons* for believing that we have the answer. So, we might put the aim of inquiry as something stronger than merely having a true belief, something like acquiring knowledge.[4] When we have knowledge, we not only have the truth, but we are tethered to it. In *Meno*, Plato (1997) uses the voice of Socrates to claim the following:

> For true opinions, as long as they remain, are a fine thing and all they do is good, but they are not willing to remain

long; and they escape from man's mind, so that they are not worth much until one ties them down by (giving) an account of the reason why ... After they are tied down, in the first place, they become knowledge, and then they remain in place.

(875)

What tethers us to the truth are our reasons. Our reasons help us grasp the truth, and they ensure that we don't give up on it, or abandon it, too easily. For instance, if someone had a true belief about the road to Larissa, they would be on the right path. But, they could easily come to have doubts or suspicions that they are on the wrong road. Without having reasons to tie them to the truth, they could easily give up their belief, even though it was true. Reasons offer a kind of stability to our beliefs. They provide security in the face of doubts that may arise.

So, we can think of inquiry as a quest to discover the answer to our question. When it comes to how to conduct our inquiry, we have two broad options. We can think for ourselves, or we can defer to someone else. Just like when we confront a home project, we have two options: DIY (the way of Rhonda) or call in the professionals (the way of Rico).

When we defer to someone else, we take their word for it. In deference, the fact that someone else said so is our reason for believing it. For instance, if my doctor tells me that I have high cholesterol, I take her word for it. I come to believe that I have high cholesterol, and I believe it because she says so. This isn't to say that I don't have any reason to trust my doctor. I have plenty of reasons to trust her. These reasons to trust her also make it reasonable for me to take her at her word. For instance, I wouldn't just believe anyone who told me I had high cholesterol, and neither should you.

While deference can come with having reasons to defer, when I defer to my doctor, I don't require seeing and evaluating the reasons that she bases her belief on in order to form my own belief. In coming to her belief that I have high cholesterol, my doctor has run various tests on me and contrasted that data with a myriad of information about other people. I could request to see all of this information and make my own determination about what it supports, but if I did that, I would no longer be deferring to my doctor, I would be thinking for myself about the issue. So, when I defer, I don't acquire or evaluate the reasons that directly support the claim in question.

It will be helpful here to distinguish two types of reasons: direct reasons and indirect reasons.[5] Direct reasons point directly to the truth of the claim in question. For instance, my memory that I had coffee this morning is a direct reason for believing that I had coffee this morning. My perceptual experience of the computer in front of me is a direct reason for believing that there is a computer in front of me. My belief that all dogs are mammals is a direct reason for believing that the next dog I see will be a mammal. In contrast, indirect reasons are reasons that are themselves *about reasons*; they are higher-order reasons. Indirect reasons are about the existence, the quantity, or the quality of reasons. So, when I tell you that I had coffee this morning, I don't give you my memory, or any other direct reason to believe that I had coffee, but I do give you reason to believe that I have such reasons. When you believe me because I told you, you believe with reason, but not with any direct reasons. Your reasons to trust me are reasons to believe that I wouldn't say so without having my own reasons to believe it. Similarly, when I tell you that I am in front of a computer, I don't thereby give you my perceptual experience of being in front of my computer. Instead, I give you reason to believe that I have my reasons for so believing. One way to think of it is as though I'm telling you that I have reasons to believe that I'm in front of my computer. In other words, I'm giving you evidence of my evidence.[6] In some sense, I'm giving you a promissory note that I have my reasons to so believe, typically without also giving you those reasons themselves. If you have good reason to trust me, then these indirect reasons are often good enough to base your belief on. It can be rational to believe me, even without getting the direct reasons on which I base my own belief.[7]

Since this distinction is important for the book, let's look at one more example. I'm a sports fan. I like to watch sports and keep up with the scores of games that I don't watch. I come to know the scores of different games in different ways. When I watch the game, I get direct reasons to believe the winning team won, and by how many points. I see for myself the reasons why they won and why they had the number of points that they had. In contrast, when I rely on a website, or an app, or a friend to tell me the score of a game, I can still come away with knowledge of the score, but only by way of indirect reasons. When a trusted sports website reports the score of a game, I can come to know that this was the score, but I don't have the direct reasons. I don't have the reasons why that was the score. I am relying on my source having those (direct) reasons and trusting that their report accurately reflects those reasons.

It is important to make the distinction between direct and indirect reasons because it would be a mistake to think that absent having direct reasons, I have *no* reasons to believe something. When you believe that I had coffee this morning on the basis of my testimony, it is not as though you have *no* reason to believe it. Rather, it is simply that you have a different *type* of reason. It's an indirect reason. So, it is important to see that indirect reasons are still reasons to believe something. That said, it is also important to see indirect reasons as distinct from direct reasons. There's an important difference between reasons to trust that someone has reasons (indirect reasons) and the reasons they have for their belief (direct reasons).

With this distinction in hand, let's return to thinking about inquiry, deference, and thinking for yourself. When I defer, I believe on the basis of indirect reasons alone; I take someone at their word. I trust that they have their reasons and that they are competent at evaluating those reasons correctly. In contrast, when I think for myself, I obtain and evaluate the direct reasons for myself. When I want to think for myself, I want to see what the reasons are that you (or my doctor) base your (or their) belief upon. I want to see those (direct) reasons, and I want to make my own evaluation of them and what they support.

We also want to distinguish how a belief was formed, and how it is sustained. Often, how a belief was formed differs from how it is sustained. For instance, when I first formed my belief that I had coffee today, it was by way of perception – I was perceiving myself drinking coffee. While I still believe that I had coffee today, what sustains that belief is not my perception. That perception is (unfortunately) long gone. Now, it is my memory that sustains my belief. So, my belief was formed on the basis of perception, but it is now maintained on the basis of memory.

This distinction is important, since whether one defers, or thinks for themselves, is not simply about how one *originally* came to the belief in question, but what sustains that belief – why they believe it *now*. If I originally believed my doctor on the basis of her say-so, but then also went on to acquire and evaluate the relevant reasons for myself, I am no longer deferring. I am no longer deferring because I am no longer simply taking my doctor at her word. While my belief originated out of deference, it is not being sustained by deference since I now believe it at least in part on the basis of the direct reasons I have evaluated.

If I am going to think for myself about whether I have high cholesterol, I will see the relevant data for myself, and I want to make my own determination about what it supports. Sandy Goldberg (2013) connects this conception of thinking for yourself with epistemic autonomy as follows:

> an epistemically autonomous subject is one who judges and decides for herself, where her judgments and decisions are reached on the basis of reasons which she has in her possession, where she appreciates the significance of these reasons, and where (if queried) she could articulate the bearing of her reasons on the judgment or decision in question.
>
> (169)

So, thinking for yourself is about having the relevant reasons, and making your own evaluation of them. Importantly, the reasons in question here are direct reasons. You can defer on the basis of indirect reasons – your reasons to trust someone else, but when you want to think for yourself, you want to see and evaluate the direct reasons yourself.

Let's revisit those initial questions. Regarding climate change, there is the testimony of climate scientists and there is the data that the climate scientists base their beliefs upon. The testimony of climate scientists provides indirect reasons to believe there is climate change. Most people believe that climate change is occurring on the basis of such indirect reasons, not on the basis of gathering the relevant direct reasons and making their own determination regarding what they support. Similar considerations apply to the benefits of flossing and the effects of caffeine. We have indirect reasons to believe these things coming from the testimony of others. Typically, we don't engage the (direct) evidence for ourselves, even if we do value thinking for yourself.

To recap, inquiry is about getting answers to our questions. We inquire to settle our questions. When we inquire, we have two choices. We can defer to someone else, or we can think for ourselves. We think for ourselves when we gather and evaluate the relevant (direct) evidence for ourselves. In contrast, when we defer, we take someone else's word for it. In deferring, we don't access the direct evidence or make our own evaluation of it.

CLARIFYING THE CENTRAL CONCLUSION

The central conclusion of this book is that it is OK not to think for yourself. This naturally invites a couple of foundational questions: What does it mean to say that something is OK? And in what sense are we saying it is OK not to think for yourself? Answering each of these will help clarify the central conclusion. Let's take them in turn. When something is OK, it is fine, or acceptable, or permissible. Importantly there is nothing wrong or inappropriate with doing things that are OK. Doing something that is OK does not entail that you couldn't have done something better.[8] Often, what it is OK to do is not what is best to do. For instance, if a dinner, or a movie, or a paper was OK, then it was perfectly fine, but it doesn't rule out that it could have been better. Saying that it is OK is simply to say that it is not defective. So, if it is OK not to think for yourself, then there is no requirement to think for yourself – thinking for yourself is not something that you must do. So much for the first question, what about the second?

We can evaluate our actions along a number of different lines. Things can be appropriate or inappropriate in many different ways. Actions could be *morally* appropriate/inappropriate, *legally* appropriate/inappropriate, *prudentially* appropriate/ inappropriate, and so forth. To say that an action is appropriate in one of these ways is not to say that it is appropriate in all of these ways. For instance, something could be legally OK without being morally OK, and vice versa. So, in what sense am I going to argue that not thinking for yourself is OK?

My main concern in this book is with the intellectual, or epistemic, appropriateness of not thinking for yourself. While the arguments advanced here also have ramifications for whether it is morally or prudentially OK for you to not think for yourself as well, my primary concern is with its epistemic permissibility. So, the arguments here are primarily concerning what can be called the ethics of belief.

Since intellectual, or epistemic, appropriateness is probably less familiar to readers than moral or prudential appropriateness, it is worth saying a little more about what it means to be intellectually appropriate. Understanding what is intellectually right/wrong and good/bad requires thinking about things from the epistemic perspective. Traditionally, we are thought to have two fundamental epistemic goals: to believe truths and to avoid believing falsehoods. These two goals keep each other in check. If our only goal was to believe truths, we would do best by believing as many things as possible. In so doing, we would end up with the greatest number of true beliefs. In contrast, if our only goal was to avoid false beliefs, we would do best by having as few beliefs as possible, since in so doing we would minimize our number of false beliefs. A healthy intellectual life requires taking both of these goals seriously.

Another way to put our epistemic goal is to have a good cognitive picture of reality. We want our minds to reflect the way that the world is. Better pictures of the world are going to be more accurate and are going to include a broader variety of claims. Our picture of the world is not only improved by adding true beliefs and limiting the false ones. Better pictures of the world also contain a variety of claims, and in particular, they contain significant truths.[9] For instance, if two people had the same number of true (and false) beliefs, while one individual's beliefs only concerned their neighborhood park and the other's beliefs concerned matters of history, art, math, literature, etc., it is clear that the latter has a better cognitive picture of the world. So, as epistemic agents, we have the goal of enhancing our cognitive picture of reality.

Returning to the central conclusion of the book, the claim is that from this *epistemic perspective*, there is nothing wrong with not thinking for yourself. Put differently, with the goal of believing truths and avoiding falsehoods, or with the goal of enhancing your cognitive picture of reality, it is perfectly fine not to think for yourself. So, the claim is that there is nothing intellectually wrong, irresponsible, or inappropriate with a kind of intellectual outsourcing.

That said, we do need to walk back this conclusion at least a little. To do so, we need to distinguish between two different types of inquirers: experts and novices. Let's start with experts. What is an expert? Experts are individuals who are well-positioned to find answers to questions, someone who is more likely to get the answer right.[10] No one is just a flat-out expert. In other words, expertise is relative to a domain, or to a set of questions. So, someone could be an expert mathematician, or an expert marine biologist, or an expert psychologist. More carefully put, then, experts are well-positioned to find answers to questions within their domain of expertise.

What makes someone well-positioned to determine an answer? Here, it is helpful to start with Goldman's account:

> Experts: people who have (or claim to have) a superior quantity or level of knowledge in some domain and an ability to generate new knowledge in answer to questions within the domain. ... [E]xperts in a given domain ... have more beliefs (or high degrees of belief) in true propositions and/or fewer beliefs in false propositions within that domain than most people do (or better: than the vast majority of people do).
>
> (Goldman 2001: 91)

On this account, experts are more reliable than non-experts in their domain of expertise, and experts also meet some threshold of reliability in that domain. So, on Goldman's account, experts have to be fairly successful at getting at the truth (and avoiding error) in their domain of expertise. What accounts for an expert's cognitive success in their domain of expertise?

Plausibly, a number of factors are relevant to one's epistemic position, or how likely one is to correctly answer a question.[11] These factors can be divided into two categories: evidential possession factors and evidential evaluation factors. Evidential possession factors concern the quantity and quality of relevant evidence that the subject possesses. Experts are informed. They have much more substantial and comprehensive bodies of evidence than non-experts. Experts have information that non-experts lack. For instance, experts on the civil war have far more information about the civil war than the rest of us. Similarly, astrophysicists have information about the universe and its workings that far outstrip common knowledge. The experts have more and better information to work with. Evidential evaluation factors concern one's ability to evaluate the evidence. Here relevant factors include cognitive abilities, time allotted to the question, and intellectual virtues. All of these features make it more likely that the expert will evaluate the body of evidence correctly. Having access to extensive bodies of evidence is of little good if you don't know how to interpret or evaluate it. For instance, expert firefighters can evaluate the scene of a fire and determine what the likely cause of the fire was, whereas those who are untrained could not make much of that very same information. Similarly, without the relevant training, looking at an MRI or CT scan won't do you much good. Complex bodies of evidence require care in evaluation. Experts can also handle the relevant evidence well. So, experts are those who are best positioned to determine answers to questions in their domain of expertise, and this is because the experts have the best information to go on, and they are best equipped to evaluate that information.

Novices are simply those that are not experts. If we are being careful, we should note that both being an expert and being a novice comes in degrees.[12] Someone can have more, or less, expertise than someone else. To the extent that someone is an expert, they are not a novice, and vice versa. We can think about how much expertise that individual has as corresponding to how good their epistemic position is on the question at hand. The better one's epistemic position, the greater their expertise. This brings out how expertise is also essentially comparative.[13] An individual's level of expertise is to be contrasted with the level of expertise of the other relevant parties. For instance, relative to my kids, I am an expert on ancient philosophy, but relative to a philosopher whose area of specialization is ancient philosophy, I am not. Again, what matters here is one's relative epistemic position – the degree to which they are more (or less) likely to be able to answer the question at hand correctly.[14] While there is an important contrastive component to expertise, it is plausible that there is also some baseline threshold that must be met. In other words, in order to be an expert, your epistemic position on the matter must meet a certain level of goodness. For instance, if you are not at all well suited to answer a question, but the rest of your community is even worse off than you are, it doesn't seem right to call you an expert on the matter.

The concern of the book is about whether you *must* think for yourself about matters where you lack expertise, about matters where you see that others are in a significantly better epistemic position to answer the question at hand than you are. I am going to argue that it's OK not to think for yourself in these situations. This isn't to say that no one should think for themselves or even that you should *never* think for yourself.

Sometimes, you are (at least roughly) as well positioned as anyone else is to answer your question. Concerning matters of your personal life history, your immediate environment, your inner life, and so forth, you have expertise. You are probably as likely as anyone to correctly answer questions in those domains.[15] Such inquiry is like Rico changing the lightbulbs in his house. Rico is as qualified as anyone is to change an easily accessible lightbulb. However, just like there is much more to house maintenance than changing lightbulbs, there are also many more questions that you seek to answer beyond these areas of your expertise.

It is important that experts think for themselves. Communities rely on their experts to find answers to questions in their respective fields of expertise, and the most reliable way to find those answers is to have the relevant experts think for themselves.[16] Our central conclusion is restricted to questions *outside* of your areas of expertise – questions where you recognize that others are more likely to be able to answer them than you are. So, we could put our central conclusion as follows: it is OK not to think for yourself when you are a novice, or it is OK not to conduct novice inquiry.

While this modification does walk the conclusion back a little, in chapter 2, I'll argue that you are often a novice. For nearly anything that you want to think about, you are aware that there is someone who is significantly better positioned to answer that question than you are. So, even with this qualification made, our central conclusion is still quite strong – it still pertains to a great deal of questions.

LOOKING AHEAD

With our central conclusion clarified, let's look at how we will get there.

In Chapter 1, I will introduce you to the notion of an epistemic surrogate. An epistemic surrogate is someone, or some group, who does your inquiry on your behalf. Epistemic surrogates carry out your inquiry and deliver you the results. I will argue that it can be rational for you to rely on epistemic surrogates. In doing so, I will look at two particularly plausible cases where this is so: one involving experts and one concerning the wisdom of crowds. In both cases, I'll argue that it can be rational to believe something just because someone else does. Put differently, having indirect reasons can be enough to make your belief rational and for you to know the answer; it can be rational for you to defer.

In Chapter 2, we will examine the first of two arguments that you don't need to think for yourself, what I'll call 'the argument from expertise.' According to the argument from expertise, for nearly anything that you want to think about, there is someone else who is significantly better at thinking about it than you are. For most questions, there is someone else who is more likely to be successful in inquiry regarding the question at hand. So, given your interest in finding the answer to your question, you are better off relying on their thinking than relying on your own. Minimally, this better alternative makes it the case that carrying out your own inquiry is unnecessary. As an intellectual agent interested in the truth, and as someone who has a better alternative available, thinking for yourself is not required.

In Chapter 3, we turn to the second argument that thinking for yourself is unnecessary, what I'll call 'the argument from evidential swamping.' According to this argument, thinking for yourself will typically not change what you are rational in believing. Rather, what it is rational for you to believe about the answer to your question will be determined by the state of the debate regarding the relevant expert opinions. If there is consensus amongst the experts, you should believe what the experts believe. If there is extensive controversy amongst the experts, then you should suspend judgment on the issue. In either case, your novice inquiry won't change what you should believe. So, since your individual inquiry will not change what it is rational for you to believe, thinking for yourself is unnecessary.

Having made the case that it is OK not to think for yourself, the rest of the book examines a number of objections to this central conclusion.

In Chapter 4, we will examine the autonomy objection. According to the autonomy objection, the life of intellectual deference conflicts with epistemic autonomy, and epistemic autonomy is too valuable to be discarded. Responding to this objection requires getting clear on what epistemic autonomy is and what it isn't. I'll argue that we should not confuse epistemic autonomy with intellectual individualism. Having distinguished two legitimate senses of epistemic autonomy, one as a kind of intellectual freedom the other as an intellectual virtue, I'll argue that neither conflicts with our central conclusion.

In Chapter 5, we will consider the free-rider objection. Free-riding occurs when someone fails to pull their own weight with respect to some common resource. According to this objection there is a shared resource, what we can call 'the epistemic commons,' and a failure to think for yourself amounts to a problematic kind of intellectual free-riding. I'll argue that while there might be something problematic about free-riding in general, there is nothing problematic about the kind of intellectual free-riding recommended by our central conclusion.

Chapter 6 concerns what I call 'the Socratic objection.' Socrates famously claimed that the unexamined life is not worth living. Along these lines, it may be thought that some questions are simply not to be outsourced; some questions simply must be thought about for oneself. Plausible examples here concern questions about morality, politics, philosophy, and religion. In response to this objection, I'll examine several possible reasons that questions in these domains are to be treated differently and argue that each of these explanations fails.

In Chapter 7, we move to the vulnerability objection. This objection claims that in deferring to others we make ourselves too intellectually vulnerable. Trust comes with vulnerability, and trusting others in inquiry leaves us vulnerable to their answers. After all, our trust can be misplaced. Further, those whom we trust can be mistaken, biased, or even manipulative. In order to protect ourselves intellectually, the objection claims, we must think for ourselves. In response to this objection, I argue that our epistemic vulnerability is inevitable. Further, contra what the objection claims, I'll argue that thinking for yourself often increases your vulnerability, not decreases it. While it is important for there to be intellectual safeguards, thinking for yourself isn't the best option here.

In Chapter 8, I consider the understanding objection. In brief, the understanding objection claims that deference is incompatible with understanding. In order to understand the answers to our questions, we must think for ourselves. Further, understanding is more valuable than anything we can gain through deference, even if we can get rational beliefs and knowledge by way of deferring. While I agree that understanding is more valuable than knowledge, and that it requires thinking for yourself, I will argue that these considerations do not show that we must think for ourselves. While it might be *better* to think for ourselves, I'll argue that it is still fine not to do so. In other words, we aren't required to do our intellectual best, and getting what we can get by deference (e.g. knowledge) is often good enough. This is a defense of epistemic satisficing.

In Chapter 9, we examine the final objection – the intellectual virtue objection. According to this objection, thinking for yourself is required to develop a good intellectual character. A good intellectual character is valuable, and this value can only be achieved by thinking for yourself. Developing as a thinker requires thinking for yourself. Use it or lose it, as they say. In response, I'll argue that a number of intellectual virtues can actually be exercised through deference. Deference can actually help us develop our intellectual character. In addition, I'll make the case that we need to revisit our list of intellectual virtues. A re-envisioned list of virtues takes social epistemology seriously and appreciates that we all have different roles to play in the informational economy.

That's the plan for the book. Is it OK not to think for yourself? In thinking about this question, you are confronted with a choice in inquiry. On the one hand, you can take my word for it, and simply believe me. In that case, you can stop now. Alternatively, you can engage in inquiry for yourself and take a look at the (direct) reasons that I have to offer throughout the book and make your own evaluation of them. Either way, I think it's OK, but for those interested in taking a look at the direct reasons, I will see you in Chapter 1.

Believing (Just) Because Other People Do

1

Most of what you believe, you believe because someone else told you so. If you were to make a list of all the things that you believe, very few would be such that you figured them out for yourself. For instance, as any successful middle schooler knows, mitochondria are the powerhouse of the cell. While you might be unsure of what exactly that means, or why you needed to learn it, you are probably sure that you simply took your teacher's word for it and didn't think about it for yourself either when you learned it, or in the time that has passed since then. Whatever the relevant direct evidence is here, you haven't looked at it yourself and you haven't made your own evaluation of it. And the lesson here generalizes. You know that Washington was the first US president, that civilization started in Mesopotamia, that our solar system started billions of years ago, and that Shakespeare wrote in English. But, for each of these beliefs, your reasons are probably entirely indirect. You haven't examined the relevant historical documents or artifacts yourself, and you haven't made the relevant calculations yourself either. None of this, however, is an indictment of you or your beliefs about these things. In particular, this does not show that these beliefs of yours are irrational. In fact, I already claimed that you *knew* all of these things. What these examples highlight is that our picture of the world relies quite heavily on others. If we had to figure everything out for

DOI: 10.4324/9781003369004-2

ourselves, our intellectual lives would be quite impoverished. Our epistemic success deeply depends on other people. If we each had to 'reinvent the wheel,' any kind of intellectual progress would never get off the ground.

The goal of this chapter is to show that it is rational to believe things on the basis of indirect reasons alone – that it can be rational to believe something just because someone else believes it. As long as you take yourself to know the claims listed at the outset of this chapter, I take it that you are already on board (at least implicitly) with this conclusion. That said, it will nevertheless be helpful to take a little bit of time explaining why this is the case and examining a couple of different ways in which it can be the case.

FROM INDIVIDUAL TO SOCIAL EPISTEMOLOGY

Epistemology is the study of knowledge and rationality. Traditionally epistemology has been quite individualistic. You are probably familiar with Descartes' famous exclamation, "I think, therefore I am." This proclamation was the foundation of his inquiry. Descartes set out to evaluate his beliefs with the goal of removing any belief that could be doubted. This method of doubt resulted in abandoning all of his beliefs that were based on perception, memory, testimony, and even rational insight. Descartes discovered that his own existence was resistant to such defeating doubt, since doubting his existence *required* his existence. Descartes had to exist in order to doubt whether he existed. Descartes thereby found his epistemological foundation, and from this foundation he set out to reassemble his cognitive picture of the world.[1]

What is relevant for our purposes is how Descartes conducted his inquiry. He did it all himself, and he did it all from his armchair. While in the end his argument relied on

God, even his reasoning about God was all done by himself and from his own perspective. This individualistic picture of inquiry has traditionally been the norm in epistemology. For instance, what it is rational for you to believe is often thought to be a matter of your evidence, what you have to go on, what sense you can make of the world from your perspective.

But, times are changing. Recently there has been a shift toward a more social conception of epistemology. Social epistemologists recognize that we are social creatures, and the effects of this fact are also seen in our intellectual lives as well. Social epistemology examines the ways in which knowledge and rationality have essentially social dimensions. Following Goldman (2011), we can delineate three main branches of social epistemology: individual social epistemology,[2] collective social epistemology,[3] and systems-oriented social epistemology. It is worth briefly commenting on each.

Individual social epistemology is concerned with the epistemic states of individuals, but with special attention being paid to the role played by 'social evidence' or what we might call 'social reasons.' Social evidence is evidence that concerns other people. This is evidence about what other people say, what they believe, what they do, and so forth. Debates within this branch of social epistemology concern questions like:

- When is it rational to believe what someone else tells you?
- Under what conditions should someone be considered an expert?
- Can it be rational to believe something when you know that others disagree?

In contrast, collective agent social epistemology concerns the epistemic states of *groups*, rather than individuals. Here, groups are taken to be the central epistemic agent. So, within this branch of social epistemology we confront questions like:

- Under what conditions does a group believe something?
- How are the beliefs of a group related to the beliefs of the members of the group?
- What makes a group's belief rational?

Finally, systems-oriented social epistemology examines and assesses the role that institutions play in our epistemic practices. Institutions affect how we come to acquire, maintain, and distribute knowledge, yet these tasks can be done better or worse. This branch of social epistemology examines which institutional arrangements work out the best in terms of our intellectual goals. Questions under this branch of social epistemology include:

- What can institutions do about the spread of fake news?
- In what ways can our scientific practices be reformed to better get at the truth?
- Do juries reach more accurate conclusions when certain types of evidence are inadmissible?

As you can see, the questions of social epistemology are broader than those of traditional individualistic epistemology.[4] The insights of social epistemology have highlighted the deep ways in which we intellectually rely on others.[5] Other people are a great intellectual resource. No one needs to go through life alone, and we can all do better when we work together. The point of this chapter is to highlight two ways in which it can be rational to rely on others. In particular, we will look at two kinds of cases where it can be rational to believe something simply because somebody else (or some group of people) does. In such cases, you are rationally believing something without having direct reasons to believe; the only reasons you have to support your belief are indirect reasons.

BELIEVING THE EXPERTS AND EPISTEMIC SURROGACY

Alongside perception, memory, and rational insight, testimony is commonly seen as one of the paradigm ways that we gain knowledge.[6] One particularly clear case of when it is rational to believe something because somebody else tells you so is when the person in question is an expert. Recall from the introductory chapter that an expert is someone who is significantly better positioned than you are to determine the answer to your question. Experts have better bodies of evidence and experts are better equipped to evaluate that evidence.

Given the nature of expertise, it is rational to defer to an expert about a matter of their expertise. Recall that you defer to someone when you believe something simply on the basis of their say-so; you don't think about it for yourself. For instance, it is rational to defer to a marine biologist about whether some fish change their sex. It is rational to defer to an economist about what percentage of the US economy is accounted for by agriculture. It is rational to defer to a historian about the number of casualties in the battle of Antietam. In each of these cases, the relevant experts have access to more, and better, information than you do, and they are well-equipped to evaluate that information. Put differently, you can do better at your goals of attaining true beliefs and avoiding false ones by deferring to the expert.[7]

Important to our point here is that it is rational to believe these experts without first acquiring and evaluating the relevant direct reasons upon which they base their beliefs.

You don't also need to conduct the relevant experiments and make the relevant observations yourself in order to come away with a rational belief or knowledge about these things. You don't also need to crunch the numbers or do the relevant calculations yourself. It is rational for you to rely on the expertise of experts. This is the role of experts within the intellectual community. If you did have to gather and evaluate all of the direct reasons for yourself, there would be no point in having the experts or specializations. In such a world, everyone could do it all for themselves, but this is not the world that we live in.

Following Grasswick (2020: 165), we can distinguish several ways in which we can trust others in inquiry. Sometimes we trust others to do the knowing for us. We trust them to find out the answers, and yet we have no expectation that they share the answers with us. In such cases, we use experts as a kind of extended mind. For instance, I might find it important that physicists are working hard on issues in quantum mechanics, but have no real interest in being kept abreast on their discoveries.[8] It is valuable for scientists to be working on cures and treatments of diseases and conditions that you don't have. In such cases you might not be interested in yourself finding out what they have discovered, but you nevertheless find it important that they are making those discoveries and advancements. So, there are cases where we trust others to inquire on our behalf with no expectation of them sharing their results with us.

Other times we trust other people in inquiry and expect them *not* to share the results of their intellectual work. Perhaps we find it important that our national intelligence agencies are conducting all kinds of covert inquiries into various international situations. However, sharing their findings publicly would conflict with the goals of national security.[9] In cases like this, we trust in inquiry while expecting not to hear the results.

However, the kind of trust in inquiry that concerns us here is when we *do* expect to hear back from the experts and for them to share their resulting knowledge with us. In this type of case, we are relying on the experts to carry out the inquiry and deliver back to us the results. In such cases, experts can act as what we might call our 'epistemic surrogates.'[10] Surrogates act on behalf of someone else. Surrogacy is most often associated with surrogate pregnancy, where an individual carries and gives birth to a child for someone else, typically someone who cannot themself give birth. The concept of epistemic surrogacy takes this idea over into the intellectual realm and concerns our intellectual projects. Epistemic surrogates carry out the inquiry on behalf of someone else, and deliver the conclusion to them, typically to someone who is not in a position to carry out the inquiry for themself. After all, no one can carry out all of the inquiries that are relevant to their lives. We all have limited time, energy, and skills. So, it is inevitable that we rely on others to conduct inquiry on our behalf. Further, many questions require specialized training to investigate. So, even if we had the time and energy to conduct the inquiry, we might not be in a position to fruitfully do so.

Unlike with surrogate pregnancy, epistemic surrogates typically do their work without any agreement or explicit directive on the part of the individual in question. We live our lives unaware of most of the inquiries that are being conducted, yet in some sense, they are being conducted on our behalf. These inquiries are being conducted to advance human knowledge. So, we benefit from the work of epistemic surrogates even when they do not act explicitly at our request. In fact, our intellectual lives are full of epistemic surrogates that have been deployed to investigate any number of questions. We can think about surrogate chemists, physicians, historians, sociologists, and political scientists. Each type of epistemic surrogate conducts inquiry in their domain of expertise on behalf of the greater public.

Let's return to our example of Rico the homeowner with the concept of surrogacy in hand. Rico employs a number of what we might call 'domestic surrogates.' These surrogates maintain Rico's property on his behalf. Rico's pool people maintain the pool on Rico's behalf. The gardener sustains the garden on Rico's behalf. Housekeepers ensure that Rico's house remains neat and tidy. Each member of the team conducts their respective set of projects on behalf of Rico. They act, in some sense, as extensions of him.

So, we trust experts to act as epistemic surrogates and conduct inquiry on our behalf. What type of reasons do we have to trust the experts and their findings? Our reasons to trust the findings of experts are indirect reasons. Since we did not also engage in the inquiry ourselves, we do not have the direct reasons that support the relevant conclusions. We don't have the same reasons that the experts have. Rather, we have indirect reasons to believe that in their inquiry, the experts obtained valuable direct reasons and have competently evaluated them. These reasons to believe that the experts have their reasons are indirect reasons, since they are reasons about reasons that we do not possess ourselves. This is one way in which these reasons are removed from us – we typically don't possess the direct reasons.

However, there is also a second way that these reasons may be removed from us. Given the nature of expertise, it could very well be that were we to come to possess the experts' reasons, we would have no idea what to make of them. Without the relevant training and expertise, we may be unable to understand the experts' reasons or be able to make any kind of determination about what they support.[11] For instance, looking at the CT scan for ourselves will do little help in determining what it supports, if we lack the training to read and evaluate such scans.

John Hardwig (1985), in his insightful essay "Epistemic Dependence," reflects on how few of his beliefs he has direct reasons to believe, and claims the following:

> Though I can readily imagine what I would have to do to obtain the evidence that would support any one of my beliefs, I cannot imagine being able to do this for all of my beliefs. I believe too much; there is too much relevant evidence (much of it available only after extensive, specialized training); intellect is too small and life too short.
>
> (335)

Michael Polanyi and Harry Prosch (1977) put the same point this way:

> The popular conception of science says that science is a collection of observable facts that anybody can verify for himself. We have seen this is not true in the case of expert knowledge, like that needed in diagnosing a disease. Moreover, it is not true in the physical sciences. In the first place, for instance, a layman cannot possibly get hold of the equipment for testing a statement of fact in astronomy or in chemistry. Even supposing that he could somehow get the use of an observatory or a chemical laboratory, he would not know how to use the instruments he found there and might very well damage them beyond repair before he had ever made a single observation; and if he should succeed in carrying out an observation to

check up on a statement of science and found a result that contradicted it, he could rightly assume that he had made a mistake, as students do in a laboratory when they are learning to use its equipment.

(184–5)

So, not only do I typically not possess the experts' (direct) reasons, but often it will be the case that even were I to come to possess them, I would be unable to make use of them as reasons. As Millgram puts it in his book *The Great Endarkment*, "we have no choice but to live together and cooperate with other individuals whom we can't possibly understand, in executing the large-scale and very demanding projects on which our survival now depends" (2015: 3).

There's a parallel point to be made in the philosophy of language. Think about the following list of terms: 'quarks,' 'anterior cruciate ligament,' 'Byzantine Empire,' 'Herbert Hoover,' 'fiber optic cable,' and 'dissociative disorders.' If you had to define each of these terms, how would you do so? If you are like me, you could probably say some true things about each of them, but probably not enough to uniquely distinguish them from other nearby concepts. In addition, there would probably be some falsehoods baked in there too. Nevertheless, you can probably competently use these terms. How can we use these terms to refer to what they refer to, when we are not able to adequately describe what they are? In cases like these, we successfully use words to refer to by intending to use them to refer to what more knowledgeable others use them to refer to. When I use the word 'quark' I want it to pick out what physicists use the term to pick out, even if I don't have a great handle on what exactly that is. You might say that I have a kind of indirect intention in my language. I intend to refer to what the relevant speakers intend to refer to in using that word. In some sense, I am off-loading my intentions and my linguistic competence onto more qualified others.

This parallels the way in which we often off-load our reasons onto the relevant experts. We may not have, or even be able to understand, the direct reasons that the experts have, but we have (indirect) reason to believe that they have them. They wouldn't be experts if they weren't in an advantageous epistemic position. Further, we can use those (indirect) reasons to justify our beliefs. Our beliefs are rational in light of the reasons that the experts have.[12]

THE WISDOM OF CROWDS

That you can rationally believe something on the basis of expert opinion is a pretty easy sell, or at least it should be. A second, and perhaps much more surprising, way that it can be rational to believe something based on what other people believe has to do with the wisdom of crowds. Often, people are scolded for believing something just because a lot of other people believe it. We're all familiar with the "and what if everyone jumped off a cliff?" way of reprimanding those who mold their behavior after the behavior of others. Regarding belief, we even have a named fallacy – the bandwagon fallacy. According to the bandwagon fallacy, or *argumentum ad populum*, it is a mistake of rationality to believe something just because many other people do. What's the problem supposed to be here? Several explanations exist, though all are lacking. Let's examine them to better understand the wisdom of crowds.

One explanation is that just because a lot of people believe something, it doesn't make it true. For instance, hundreds of years ago lots of people believed that the Earth was flat and yet it never was. The shape of the Earth has never been determined by the beliefs of its inhabitants. Similarly, people believing that God exists does not make it the case that God exists. Whether or not God exists, it is not the opinions of people that make it the case one way or the other. That's all fine and good, but it would be pretty silly to think that such a confusion is going on when people believe something because others do. It is unlikely that people are thinking that the beliefs of others is what is making their belief true.

A second, and related, explanation of the badness of the bandwagon fallacy is that when you believe something just because other people do, you don't believe it for the reasons that make it true. This explanation doesn't require that anyone thinks that peoples' beliefs make their beliefs true, it simply claims that since beliefs don't make things true, believing on this basis is the wrong type of reason. One way to understand this explanation is to think of it as claiming that indirect reasons aren't the right kind of reasons; that indirect reasons can't make a belief rational. There are several problems with this explanation though. First, if indirect reasons couldn't make a belief rational, then this would apply equally well to beliefs based on expert testimony. As we've seen, this is a non-negotiable. Clearly, we can rationally believe things on the basis of expert testimony. In addition, in complaining that the reasons why you believe something are not the reasons why it is true, this explanation confuses two types of reasons: epistemological reasons and metaphysical reasons. Metaphysical reasons concern why something is the case. For instance, causes are metaphysical reasons for their effects. Metaphysical reasons are about why the world is the way that it is, they are about what is going on in the world out there outside of our minds. In contrast, epistemological reasons are reasons to believe that something is the case. Epistemological reasons concern what it is rational to believe about the world. Epistemological reasons and metaphysical reasons are importantly different kinds of reasons, even if both are a type of reasons.

Importantly, that a given reason isn't a metaphysical reason does not show that it is not an epistemological reason. For instance, my perceptual experience of there being a computer in front of me is an epistemological reason for my believing that there is a computer in front of me; it gives me a good reason to believe that there is a computer there. However, my perceptual experience is not a metaphysical reason. My perceptual experience is not what *made it the case* that there is a computer in front of me. There is a computer in front of me because of all kinds of reasons including my desires and intention to write this book, but my perceptual experience isn't one of these reasons. Perceptions don't cause the states in the world that are being perceived. However, noting that my perceptual experience is not a reason why there is a computer in front of me does not indicate that my perceptual experience is not an epistemological reason for believing there is a computer in front of me. My perceptual experience is still what makes my computer belief rational. This is a clear case where an epistemological reason is not a metaphysical reason. So, the fact that the beliefs of others do not make their beliefs true (that they aren't metaphysical reasons), does not show that they can't make the belief in question reasonable (that they are not epistemological reasons). This explanation of the problem with the bandwagon fallacy simply rests on a confusion.

A third cited problem with the alleged fallacy is that in believing what others believe, you could still get it wrong. You could believe what lots of people believe, and nevertheless still end up with a false belief. The fact that many people believe something is no guarantee that it is true. Again, if you believed that the Earth was flat because everyone you knew believed the Earth was flat, you ended up with a false belief. So, the majority can be wrong.

While that's true, only the radical skeptic thinks that the mere possibility of error is a strong enough reason to abandon a certain type of thinking or to treat it as fallacious. After all, our perception can get it wrong, our memories can be mistaken, we can even be let down by what seems like rational insight. Returning to the first half of this chapter, the experts can be wrong too. If the mere possibility of error prevents something from being a good reason, then we aren't left with many reasons. Very few of our reasons offer guarantees.

So, either we endorse widespread skepticism, or we embrace the idea that many great reasons simply don't guarantee the truth of what they support. That is, good reasons can still be *fallible reasons*. Fallible reasons are reasons that are consistent with the falsity of what they are reasons for. My perceptual experience of a computer in front of me is a fallible reason for believing that there is a computer in front of me. While it is a good reason, my perceptual experience is still consistent with there being no computer in front of me. After all, I could be dreaming, hallucinating, being deceived by an evil demon, or I could be a brain-in-a-vat. Similar things are true of the reasons I get from memory, introspection, testimony, and rational insight. So, using fallible reasons isn't fallacious reasoning. If it was, nearly all of our reasoning would be fallacious, and the radical skeptic would be right. So, this explanation of the bandwagon fallacy also fails.

What then could be the problem with the bandwagon fallacy? I'm going to argue that nothing needs to be wrong with reasoning in this way. Put differently, you can rationally come to a belief just because you are aware that lots of other people believe it. Hilary Kornblith (2010) agrees, claiming that, "one would have to be a radical skeptic about mathematics, logic, probability, and decision theory to think that convergence of opinion is not, at this point in the history of those fields, evidence of truth" (40–1).

Let's look at a concrete example to help make the point. I could rationally come to believe that the recycling is getting picked up today simply on the basis of discovering that a bunch of my neighbors believe that today is recycling day. Let's see why. Suppose that one morning as I go to get into my car, I notice that many of my neighbors have their recycling bins on the road. Since the Homeowners Association (HOA) gets very upset if people leave their recycling bins out, this leads me to believe that these neighbors all believe that the recycling is getting picked up today. It seems that I could reason as follows:

1. Many people in my neighborhood believe that the recycling is getting picked up today.
2. The recycling getting picked up today is a good explanation of why so many people in my neighborhood believe that it is.
3. The recycling being picked up today better explains why so many people in my neighborhood believe this than any available rival explanation.
4. So, the recycling is getting picked up today.[13]

It is reasonable for me to believe premise (1) since I see so many recycling bins on the road. My neighbors wouldn't put their recycling out if they did not believe that today was recycling day. After all, no one wants to get hounded and fined by the HOA. So, (1) is reasonable to believe.

We can then ask why so many of my neighbors believe this. Here are several alternative explanations on offer:

1. The recycling is getting picked up today.
2. Most of my neighbors are mistaken about what day it is.
3. A mischievous individual, who sent most of my neighbors fake recycling date change notifications, has deceived them.
4. Most of my neighbors have excessive recycling and really want it to be picked up today, and this desire has caused them to believe that it will be picked up today.[14]

Each of these four alternatives can explain why so many of my neighbors believe that the recycling is being picked up today. However, they don't all do so equally well. It's pretty clear that (A) is by far the best explanation of the lot. While any one of my neighbors could be confused about what day it is, the odds that so many of them were all confused, and confused in the same way, is highly unlikely. Similarly, while it is entirely possible that there was this mischievous individual who decided to prank the neighborhood, this explanation doesn't fit too well with all of my background knowledge. The possibility that my neighbors believe this because of wish-fulfillment is also possible, but very unlikely. In contrast, if today is recycling day, it would make a lot of sense for many of my neighbors to be aware of that and thereby believe it. So, not only is (A) a better explanation of my neighbors' beliefs than (B), (C), or (D), it's also a really good explanation. These considerations make both premises (2) and (3) reasonable to believe. On this basis, it looks perfectly reasonable for me to conclude that today is recycling day. In fact, it is unlikely that I would need to explicitly go through such reasoning to make my recycling belief reasonable. Usually, whatever inference there is happens quite quickly and mostly under the level of consciousness. That said, it is still helpful to make the reasoning explicit and see how it is in fact a good way to reason.

So, here too, we have an instance where it is reasonable for an individual to believe something based solely on the fact that other people believe it. Importantly, I am reasonable in believing that today is recycling day without first gathering all of the relevant direct reasons that each of my neighbors have. I don't need to knock on doors and ask each individual neighbor why they believe that today is recycling day. I can reasonably hold my belief without having the direct reasons that my neighbors base their beliefs upon. My indirect reasons suffice to make my belief rational. It's enough that I have good reason to believe that they have their reasons.[15]

This result can be further supported by looking at the Condorcet Jury Theorem. According to the Condorcet Jury Theorem, the majority opinion becomes more and more likely to be correct as more independent individual opinions are added into the mix, so long as the individuals are each more likely than not to be correct. For instance, in a group of 250 people who are each individually only 0.51 likely to be correct on some matter, the majority opinion is 0.62 likely to be correct. In a group of 10,000 people with that same small likelihood of getting it right, the majority opinion leaps to a whopping 0.98 likelihood of being correct![16] So, a majority belief can provide quite powerful reasons to believe.

We can appreciate the idea here without getting too bogged down in the formal details of the Condorcet Jury Theorem. Many of you are probably familiar with the trivia gameshow *Who Wants to be a Millionaire?* The show was incredibly popular in the early 2000s. In it, contestants were given a series of ever increasingly difficult multiple-choice questions which ended with the possibility of winning a million dollars. To aid them on their quest, contestants were given three lifelines. These lifelines were i) the 50/50, where half of the answers were removed, ii) phone a friend, where the player could reach out for help from a knowledgeable friend, and iii) ask the audience, where the audience would be polled on the same question and the contestant could see how they answered. As the data has been analyzed over the years, it has become clear that polling the audience is a much more effective lifeline than calling an expert-friend. According to Surowiecki (2004), the expert-friend had around a 65% chance of getting the answer correct, while the answer that was given by a majority of the studio audience was correct 91% of the time![17] So, while relying on an expert-friend was a good strategy, there was far more wisdom in the majority opinion of a somewhat random group of strangers. In addition, whereas when a contestant phoned a friend, they could hear their friend's reasoning and why they thought a certain answer was correct, when the contestant used the ask the audience lifeline instead, all they got was a report on the beliefs of the audience members. Contestants did not get to hear why any audience members thought that their answer was correct. So, the only reasons the ask the audience lifeline presented were indirect reasons, yet here too these reasons were quite powerful.

This is just one example of the work that social scientists have been doing concerning the wisdom of crowds.[18] Other cases show how group judgments can be more accurate than individual judgments. Surowiecki begins his 2004 book, *The Wisdom of Crowds*, with the example from Sir Francis Galton. Galton had collected data from 787 people at the 1906 West of England Fat Stock and Poultry Exhibition, who each guessed the weight of an ox. In compiling the guesses, Galton found that the average guess was 1,197 pounds, only one pound off from the actual weight of the ox! Along these lines, Cass Sunstein (2008) describes how when a group of 56 individuals guessed the number of beans in a jar, their average guess (871) was closer to the correct answer (850) than all but one of the individual guesses. What this research shows is that relying on what the majority in a group believes can be a reliable way to go. Further, relying on group opinions has become an increasing part of our lives. When we go to decide which movie to see, which nearby restaurant we should visit, which electrician to call, or which blender to buy, we often rely on the reports of the beliefs of others. A movie's Rotten Tomatoes score, a restaurant's Yelp rating, an electrician's rating on Angie's List, and a blender's Amazon star rating all give feedback about the beliefs of others. This information can be incredibly helpful in navigating the world and making informed decisions.

The rough idea here should make sense. Individuals have different backgrounds, they have different biases, blindspots, experiences, and insights. When you aggregate the views of diverse people, you are likely to converge on the truth. These biases and blindspots are likely to cancel-out since it is unlikely that a diverse group will all be biased in the same way or have the same blindspots. Further, if their individual distinct bodies of evidence point to the same truth, that is a good indication of the truth of the claim in question.

None of this is to say that it is always rational to go with popular beliefs. For instance, according to IMDb voters,[19] *The Shawshank Redemption* is the greatest movie of all time. While *The Shawshank Redemption* is no doubt a great movie, it is hard to believe it is the greatest of all time. Further, the fact that a given presidential candidate wins the popular vote does not make it rational to believe that they are best suited to lead the country. There are plenty of examples here. So, adopting the majority's belief is not always rational. What then explains the difference between the good cases and the bad cases? There are several important factors that are relevant here. First, it is important that the individual beliefs in question are independent. If there are strong social or political pressures to believe something, then the truth of that belief will not be the best explanation of why so many people believe it. Let's start with an extreme case. Suppose there is a dictator who regularly polls his citizens as to whether he is the greatest dictator of all time. Those who disagree are immediately killed. In this state, the belief that this dictator is the greatest of all time might be quite prevalent. It will at least appear like everyone believes it. However, we have a better explanation for this convergence of opinion. The fear of death is a better explanation of why everyone believes (or at least reports that they believe) this than is the truth of their beliefs.

Similarly, let's alter our recycling case. Suppose that Susan is the neighbor that everyone looks up to. Everyone in the neighborhood wants to be like Susan. When Susan plants roses, most of the neighborhood ends up planting roses. When Susan puts out holiday decorations, most of the neighbors follow suit. Now I come to learn that most of my neighbors believe that the recycling is being picked up today. In this revised case, there is at least a strong competitor explanation for the prevalence of this recycling belief. It could be that most of the neighbors acted in this way, and believed this, just because Susan did. If so, then their collective beliefs will count for much less of a reason to believe that it is recycling day. So, independence of opinion is one significant factor.

Another significant factor is reliability. If the individuals in question are each unlikely to be able to determine the answer, then the fact that there is a shared majority opinion amongst them won't count for much. If I survey a class of elementary students about which theory of quantum mechanics is correct, the fact that the majority believe it is the many worlds interpretation won't give me reason to agree with them. Aggregating unreliable opinions isn't a good way to go. So, competence is an important factor as well.

What it all comes down to is the question of what best explains the convergence of opinion. Sometimes the best explanation will be social pressure.[20] Sometimes no explanation will look very good. However, sometimes the truth of the belief in question will not only best explain why so many people believe it, it will also be quite a good explanation of that fact. When that is the case, we have good reason to believe in line with the group.

The fact that there are bad cases might show that there is something right about the bandwagon fallacy after all. Such reasoning at least *can* go awry. Perhaps it even goes awry more often than not. That is, perhaps as a matter of fact, there are more bad cases than good cases of such reasoning. However, what we have seen is that the diagnosis of the problem is not simply that someone is believing something because most other people do. A better diagnosis of the problem needs to be much more fine-grained than anything given in the named fallacy itself. In particular, it needs to address what best explains why so many people believe the claim in question. As we have seen, sometimes it can be that it is the truth of their belief that is the best explanation.

The point relevant to our purposes here is only that it *can* be rational to believe something just because other people do.

It is certainly not the case that we are *always* rational in so doing, and I don't want to make any commitments regarding exactly how frequently the types of cases we have in mind come up. Appealing to the wisdom of crowds simply shows one additional way in which it can be rational to believe something on the basis of indirect reasons alone. In such cases, your reason for believing the claim in question is that so many other people believe it. You have reason to believe that they have good reasons for their beliefs. While you lack their direct reasons, your indirect reasons are sufficient to give you a reasonable belief.

THE UPSHOT

Let's slightly reframe the upshot of this chapter. You don't need to think for yourself to come away with a rational belief or even knowledge. You can know things even when the relevant inquiry has been outsourced to others. One way to rationally outsource inquiry is to rely on the epistemic surrogacy of experts. In doing so, you trust experts to carry out the relevant inquiry and deliver the results to you. Another way to rationally outsource inquiry is to rely on the wisdom of crowds. When the best explanation of the prevalence of a belief is its truth, then it is rational for you to believe it even without having the direct reasons on which others hold their beliefs. So, you don't need to gather the direct reasons and evaluate them for yourself in order to come away with a rational belief or knowledge. In some sense, that should be obvious. If thinking for yourself was the only route to knowledge, a radical and widespread skepticism would ensue. While I take it that the central point of this chapter is fairly obvious, it does set us up to confront a troubling problem. Since we don't need to think for ourselves in order to get a rational belief or knowledge, what then is the point of thinking for ourselves? What makes this question more pressing is that often it is the case that we will do much better at answering our questions by *not* thinking for ourselves – this leaves thinking for yourself unnecessary. That's the argument from expertise, and it will be our focus in the next chapter.

The Argument from Expertise

2

In the last chapter, we saw that it can be rational to defer; that it can be rational to take someone else's word for it and believe something on indirect reasons alone. In this chapter, we will build on that point in constructing our first of two arguments that thinking for yourself is often unnecessary; that in many cases it's OK not to. Remember that by 'thinking for yourself' we mean gathering the relevant direct evidence and making your own evaluation of it. So, when it comes to answering a question, deference and thinking for yourself are distinct options. This first argument, the argument from expertise, claims that thinking for yourself is often unnecessary since there is typically a better way for you to go about finding the answer to your question. For almost any question you want to answer, someone else is going to be better at finding the answer. Given that you often have this better alternative, thinking for yourself is often unnecessary.

We can put the argument from expertise as follows:

1. For nearly any question that you may have, there is a better available route to the answer than thinking about it for yourself.

2. If there is a better available route to the answer than thinking about it for yourself, then thinking about it for yourself is unnecessary.

DOI: 10.4324/9781003369004-3

3. So, for nearly any question you want to answer, thinking about it for yourself is unnecessary.[1]

MOTIVATING THE ARGUMENT

Let's look at our premises one at a time. What about premise (1)? Well, for nearly anything that you want to think about, you are aware that someone else is better positioned to determine the answer to your question than you are. Put differently, for almost any question you might have, someone else is more likely to uncover the answer than you are. Recall that what improves one's epistemic position, what makes it more likely that they will be correct, has to do with the evidence that they possess and their ability to evaluate that evidence. So, for almost all of your questions, there is someone else who has better evidence than you do, and is better qualified to evaluate the relevant evidence than you are. Alternatively, very few questions are such that you are just about as well suited as anyone else is to find the answer. Don't worry, you are not alone here. This is true of all of us. Given our intellectual goals of believing truths and avoiding falsehoods, thinking for yourself is often an inferior option in inquiry. If we are after the truth, there is typically a better alternative to finding it.

Sometimes, your epistemic position is about as good, or better, than anyone else's. Regarding your own personal history, or your immediate environment, you might be as well positioned as anyone else is to answer your questions. Questions in this category might consist of the following:

- What did I have for breakfast this morning?
- Are they any dogs in this room?
- Do I have a headache now?
- How long have I lived in my current home?

For questions like these, you are probably as likely as anyone else is to know the answer. However, questions like these are but a very small fraction of the questions that you confront or are interested in answering. Once we start thinking about things beyond our own personal lives and immediate environment, it is easy to see that others are often much better positioned than we are to answer these questions. Other people are more intelligent, have better evidence, have thought about it longer, and so forth. Even if you have expertise beyond your personal history and environment, for most things that you may want to think about, you are not an expert, and you are aware that others are.

Let's revisit our analogy with Rico the homeowner. What is true of us in inquiry is also true of Rico with regard to home maintenance. For nearly any home project that Rico may want to take on, he is aware that there is someone else who is better equipped at successfully taking on that project. Sure, when it comes to changing lightbulbs, or taking out the trash, Rico is as capable as anyone else is, but once we move beyond such small tasks, there are almost always others with more experience, training, and requisite skills that make their success at the project more likely than Rico's. Of course, outsourcing these projects comes at a financial cost to Rico, but setting financial incentives aside, and thinking only about what course of action is most likely to result in successful home maintenance, outsourcing is often the way to go for Rico. Insofar as Rico is simply interested in getting the job done well, he should have someone who is better equipped to perform the task do it. Minimally, the fact that others are better at the task at hand shows that he isn't required to do the maintenance himself. He can't be required to take on the project when he has a better option available.

This is why we hire plumbers and electricians to solve our plumbing and electrical problems. While we could try and solve our plumbing or electrical problems ourselves, at least for most of us, we are well aware of our limitations and that others are much more likely to succeed at these tasks. As long as we are not plumbers or electricians ourselves, we are aware that others are much better suited to solve our plumbing and electrical problems. Given our interest in resolving such issues, it makes sense to take the course of action that is more likely to succeed in solving the problem. And, almost always, that course of action involves outsourcing our repairs, and that is so even when it comes with additional financial cost. There is nothing wrong or irresponsible with having some-one else take on the project. In fact, that is precisely what someone who cares about getting the job done would do.

Let's return to our intellectual projects. In our intellectual projects, we have the goal of figuring out the answers to our questions. The goal of inquiry is to know the answer; to figure out the fact of the matter. Like with the home repair analogy, there are better and worse routes to this goal. Not all alternatives come with the same likelihood of success. We could conduct our own individual inquiry, or we could outsource the investigation to someone else. Since, for most questions, we know that there is someone else who is better positioned to determine the answer, for most of our questions, inquiry is more likely to be successful if we outsource it. Often, we are better off relying on someone else to determine the answer to our question. So much for premise (1). It is hard to deny for anyone with an ounce of intellectual humility.

What about premise (2)? Once we realize that outsourcing our inquiry gives us a better chance at answering our question, thinking for ourselves becomes unnecessary. When there is a better alternative available, we should take it. At the very least, it wouldn't be wrong or inappropriate to go with this better alternative. Remember that our intellectual goals are to believe truths and avoid believing falsehoods. There is nothing wrong with taking the options in inquiry that maximize our chances of success along these lines. If anything, doing so is exactly the thing that we should be doing.

For instance, suppose that we are trying to determine whether a given liquid is an acid or a base, and that we have two tools at our disposal. The first is litmus paper. Litmus paper is paper treated with dyes to indicate whether a liquid is an acid or a base. While it is a very reliable indicator, it isn't perfect. Other chemical reactions can cause the litmus paper to change color. The second device that we have at our disposal is a homemade test that I have devised. I haven't had time to run trials on my device, so there is no indication of how accurate it is. My device certainly hasn't gone through the tests, revisions, and refinements that litmus paper has. With our interest in discovering whether the liquid in question is an acid or a base, which tool should we use? It seems clear that we should opt for using the litmus paper. The litmus paper is a proven, highly reliable method for answering the question at hand, whereas my homemade device is not. Going with the litmus paper is the way to go.

To take another example, suppose that you have a friend who is making plans for a picnic this week and they are curious about what the weather will be like on Tuesday. They have the opportunity to consult one of their leading local meteorologists, Briana Breeze, or they can think about things for themselves. No meteorologist is perfect, but let's suppose that Briana Breeze is a pretty reliable predictor of the weather. In contrast, the relevant meteorological data is vast, complex, and difficult for a novice to interpret. Relevant data includes satellite imagery, radar data, radiosonde data, upper-air data, wind profilers, and so forth. Predicting the weather from that data requires being able to identify different patterns and monitor for minute changes. Given this, novice interpretation of the data is unlikely to yield the correct verdict. Your friend might be curious to see the relevant data, but insofar as they are simply interested in getting Tuesday's weather right, they should listen to Briana Breeze. Listening to Briana presents their better opportunity at getting Tuesday's weather right. After all, Briana is the expert, and they are just a novice.

While this point might be easy to see from the third-person perspective, notice, however, that this same conclusion holds for you, and I, as well. If it was *you* that was planning the picnic, you too are better off relying on Briana Breeze's forecast than you are in thinking about it for yourself. And the same goes for me. Here too, you might be curious and simply want to think about it for yourself, but insofar as you simply desire to get to the truth about the weather, relying on Briana is the better bet. Relying on Briana's inquiry is a better way to fulfil your intellectual goals than relying on your own novice inquiry.

While these cases might show that it is valuable to listen to the experts, we might need to say more about why we need not at least *also* think for ourselves. Isn't an even better option to listen to the experts *and* think about things for yourself? It might be thought that in doing both you can increase your odds of getting at the truth, but that's not the case. Adding novice inquiry to expert inquiry will not significantly improve our odds of intellectual success and it comes with some potential dangers. To see this, let's turn to a new analogy.

Suppose that you have been selected to compete on a competitive baking show.[2] Having passed through the first several rounds of the competition you are faced with a final challenge – an intricate and complicated dessert. The task is daunting for you since you are not an expert baker. However, this competition does grant you a lifeline. Martha Stewart is on standby, and if beckoned, she will take on the task for you. Martha Stewart is an expert baker and her success at this task is much more likely than yours. With the interest of successfully completing the task, should you take on the project yourself or outsource it to Martha? It seems clear that given the opportunity to use this lifeline you should take it. Having Martha take her crack at the dessert is your best bet for success. If either of you can do it, it is Martha. If it is something that she can do, then you are better off letting her do it. If it is something that is even too complicated for Martha, you are still better off letting her give it her best shot. Either way, your odds improve by turning the project over to Martha.

Now, there is a third option. You could *both* attempt it. However, so long as Martha is already giving it a go, your odds of success do not increase in any significant way by you also taking a crack at it. If anything, your added attempt will only get in Martha's way and bring down her odds of success. So, your best bet is to turn over the project entirely.

This lesson also applies to our homeowner analogy. So long as Rico has decided to outsource the electrical repairs to a qualified electrician, Rico *also* attempting the repairs is not going to significantly increase the odds of a successful repair, and if anything, it seems that his so doing will actually lower the chances of the repairs being successfully completed.

So, in both of these practical analogues, the 'both/and' path appears to not be a better option. So long as you are going to outsource the project, you also taking it on yourself appears to be unnecessary and perhaps even problematic.

Does this conclusion carry over to our intellectual projects? I think so. Let's revisit our litmus paper case. While we saw that we should use the litmus paper, we might wonder why we should not also use my homemade device. We might want to use my device as well out of pure curiosity, but let's think about how things may go. Suppose my homemade device gave the same verdict as the litmus paper. That would be a win for my device, but it wouldn't make it any more likely that the litmus paper's verdict was correct. The reading from my device wouldn't boost our reasons for believing the litmus paper. Alternatively, if my device gave a reading contrary to what the litmus paper claimed, then it wouldn't become any less reasonable to believe the litmus paper. All that result would do would give us reason to believe that my homemade device is no good. So, using my homemade device would not improve our reasons for believing the answer given by the litmus paper. Similar considerations apply to the picnic case. A novice evaluation of the evidence won't significantly strengthen or weaken the reasons to trust Briana Breeze.

Here is how Hardwig (1994) makes this point:

> Within her area of expertise, an expert's opinion is better than a non-expert opinion. By 'better,' I mean more reliable. ... Areas in which expert opinion exists and is available are areas in which one ought not to make up one's own mind – without first becoming an expert.
>
> (84–5)

Hardwig, and a number of other philosophers,[3] have argued that the considerations that motivate the argument from expertise have it that novices should not be conducting their own inquiry – that novices should *not* think for themselves.[4] Millgram (2015) puts it this way: "when it comes to just about anything that really matters, [thinking for yourself] is no longer an option: that no matter how resolute or courageous you are, you have to let others do most of your thinking for you." (35)

The conclusion I am after here is significantly weaker. Our conclusion is simply that it is *not necessary* to think for yourself – that it is OK not to, at least when you are not yourself an expert. So, our conclusion does not maintain that novices do anything wrong when they also think for themselves, it simply claims that it is perfectly fine to refrain from conducting their own inquiry.

Given all of this, premise (2) also looks quite plausible. When there is a better available route to the answer, you don't need to think for yourself. This matters since we have seen with premise (1) that there is usually a better way to answer your questions than by thinking for yourself. It follows that there is typically nothing wrong with not thinking for yourself. If both premises (1) and (2) are correct, then we should also endorse the conclusion, (3), that for nearly any question, thinking for yourself is unnecessary.

Having motivated the argument from expertise, let's turn to look at how it applies to cases. In seeing its application, we can gain further support for the conclusion that thinking for yourself is often unnecessary.

APPLYING THE ARGUMENT

Consider the following cases. Each further makes plausible the claim that thinking for yourself is often unnecessary since there is typically a better route to the answer.

THE GREAT ONE: On his morning commute, Stan is listening to his favorite sports talk radio show. He hears that even if Wayne Gretzky did not score any of his record 894 goals, he would still be the NHL point leader in virtue of the assists that he had. Stan is amazed, but he believes the statistic. While Stan might look it up later (and thereby verify with other expert opinions), it would be silly for Stan to collect all of the relevant direct evidence himself (for instance, to go watch all of the relevant games for himself or look at all the box scores) in order to determine for himself whether the stat is correct.[5] While that is one way for Stan to live his life, epistemically speaking, it would be a waste of his time. Since he has credible testimony, a true belief, a rational belief, and knowledge are all his for the taking without these efforts. Thinking for himself would be [a] waste. It wouldn't improve anything, and if anything, Stan would make a mistake in his calculations and end up being led away from the truth.[6]

CAFFEINE: Luna has recently become very interested in nutrition. Recently, she has been studying caffeine and its effects on the body. In her inquiry, Luna consults her chemist friend Cora who tells her, among other things, that caffeine has the molecular formula $C8H10N4O2$. This is new information to Luna, but Luna is aware that Cora knows her stuff. Instead of simply taking Cora's word for it, Luna could try and figure out the molecular formula of caffeine for herself. All she would need to do is find the molar mass of the compound, divide it by the empirical formula mass, and so forth. However, Luna recognizes that she is far more likely to bungle these measurements and calculations than she is to do it all correctly. If anything, thinking for herself here would only lead her away

Why It's OK Not to Think for Yourself

from the answer that she has by way of her trusted chemist friend Cora.[7]

HAMILTON: Mya has recently watched the musical *Hamilton*. Since then, she has been fascinated with the life of Eliza Hamilton. In reading a biography about the Hamiltons, Mya discovers that Eliza and Alexander had eight children. This is news to Mya since it isn't represented in the musical. Mya could look into the matter for herself, digging up documents, recreating the family trees, and so forth, but now that she knows this about Eliza from the biography, further inquiry seems to be superfluous at best. There is nothing wrong with her believing the biography and not thinking about it for herself.

MASKING: In the middle of the recent pandemic, Raymond is curious as to whether masks are effective in slowing the spread of COVID. There are two different ways that Raymond could go about answering his question. One option is to defer to the relevant experts, like those at the Center for Disease Control, and believe that wearing a mask is an effective step in protecting yourself (and others) against COVID on the basis of their say-so. Alternatively, Raymond could do his own research. He could run his own experiments about the effectiveness of masks, or he could gather the results of all the other research that has already been conducted, and evaluate those results for himself. Raymond may be curious about the particular findings, but he doesn't need to see them for himself. He is reasonable in believing the experts and deferring to their judgment. Doing his own research is unnecessary.

DIAGNOSIS: You haven't been feeling well recently. Something is off, and you are interested in discovering what it is so that you can fix it. One option is to go to your doctor and have your doctor examine you, run some tests, and come up with a diagnosis. A second option is self-diagnosis. You could do your own research and draw your own conclusions about what ails you. The first option is a far superior one. Doctors have medical expertise, and medical expertise matters. Doctors have seen a lot and they can pick up on subtleties that can easily be missed by an untrained eye. Put differently, they are in a much better epistemic position to determine the problem. In contrast, self-diagnoses don't have a great track record.[8] We are probably all familiar with a friend who has Googled their symptoms and come away with a wild diagnosis. Here, too, thinking for yourself is at best unnecessary and at its worst, dangerous.

Now let's draw some morals from these cases. In each of these cases our subject confronts a dilemma in inquiry. They could defer to the relevant expert, or they could (at least also) think about the matter for themselves. What these cases make clear is that thinking about it for themselves is not necessary. There is no intellectual requirement here to do so. In each case, our subject has access to an individual who is in a far superior epistemic position on the matter at hand – someone who is far more likely to arrive at the fact of the matter than they are on their own. If anything, to ignore this better option in order to take the much less reliable route of individual inquiry would be intellectually irresponsible. To supplement the expert opinion with one's own research would minimally be unnecessary, but it might even get in the way of their intellectual goals. Since the subjects in our cases are not themselves experts in the relevant domains, they are not particularly likely to be successful at carrying out their own inquiry. So, adding their own inquiry into the mix is not going to result in improved odds at discovering the answer, and it may even interfere.

While we have only looked at five cases, the lessons here seem to generalize. The content of these cases is diverse, and there do not appear to be any unique features that distinguish these cases from the other kinds of inquiry that we engage. That said, in Chapter 6 we will examine an objection to our central conclusion that the lesson from these cases fails to generalize to a significant set of inquiries. So, we will return to this issue later, but at least for now, we will treat our set of cases as representative.

AN INITIAL WORRY: IDENTIFYING THE EXPERTS

At this point, a worry may have emerged. Even if you are entirely on board with the point being argued here, you might nevertheless worry that it is impractical. That is, you might doubt that the advice given here is very useful. Sure, you might think, we should listen to the experts, but finding the experts is no easy task. If we can't figure out who the experts are, then deferring to them isn't really a viable option after all. Expert inquiry is only available to us if we can identify who the relevant experts are.

To further motivate this worry, we should note that we live in a highly specialized world. While this fact makes expertise important, it can also make it harder to identify who the relevant experts are, particularly when you yourself are not an expert in that field. For instance, from my perspective, an actual expert astrophysicist and an imposter might sound equally credible. I might have a hard time making sense of what either of them are saying, and it may feel as if each is speaking a foreign language. The foreign language analogy is apt. If you don't speak Thai, then you will likely have a very hard time distinguishing a native Thai speaker from an imposter (at least one who has been practicing at playing the part). Outsiders can have a hard time differentiating the good cases from the bad cases. Elijah Millgram (2015: 45) acknowledges this worry, noting that often, "in order to apply the standards of the __ologists, you have to be a __ologist yourself."

So, what can be said in response to this worry? I want to outline several distinct responses that one might have, each of which will still make the rest of the book worth reading.

According to the first response, the pessimistic response, we can concede that there are cases where expert identification is simply too difficult for novices to make. In such cases, our central conclusion simply won't apply. You should defer to the experts when you can, but if you can't figure out who the experts are, or what they believe, this advice just doesn't apply. This concessive response grants our objector's point, but notes that there are still many cases where we *can* identify who the relevant experts are, and in those cases, our central conclusion still applies. Put differently, pointing out that there are cases where we cannot identify the experts doesn't render our conclusion insignificant if there are still plenty of cases where we can do so. Whenever we can identify the experts, there is no problem with outsourcing our inquiry.

The second response is more ambitious and more optimistic than the first. According to the second response, we shouldn't be so pessimistic about our abilities to identify the relevant experts. In filling out this response, it will be helpful to look at some of the strategies for expert identification that have been given in the literature.[9]

1 Track-Records

In some domains, the claims of putative experts are frequently put to the test. This results in their having a track-record which gives evidence of their reliability.[10] For instance, while it might be difficult as a non-meteorologist to distinguish a genuine meteorology expert from an imposter, with weather predictions comes a track-record. If someone is routinely getting things wrong, and wildly wrong, then we have good reason to believe that they are not an expert. On the other hand, if someone is able to make quite accurate predictions about the weather, then we have reason to believe that they are an expert. Just like a trusted electrician or plumber will rely on their track-record, kinds of cognitive expertise can be determined on the basis of a history of correct judgments.[11]

There are limitations here. Not every domain comes with predictions that can be easily determined, particularly by someone who is not themselves an expert in the field. While you don't have to be a meteorologist to determine whether it is raining, assessing the predictions of astrophysicists is another matter altogether. In addition, other domains aren't predictive in the relevant sense at all. Determining the track-record of a philosopher, a historian, or a sociologist is not an easy feat, even for those who have expertise in the relevant domains.[12]

2 Indirect Calibration

Another way to identify experts in a domain is to rely on experts in nearby domains.[13] Domains of inquiry often overlap. That is, experts in different domains are sometimes inquiring about the same, or at least nearby, questions. In cases like these, we have the added resource of looking at what experts in the neighboring domain say about the experts in the target domain. If it is easier to identify the experts in the neighboring domain, then this will facilitate our identification of experts in the target domain. As Nguyen (2018b) puts it:

> Fields overlap. If I trust the engineers, and engineering substantially overlaps with mathematics, then I can trust the engineers via a litmus test, and then trust the mathematicians via the engineers. Nuclear engineering has a fairly vivid litmus test, and the field depends on the results of theoretical physics. Thus, my trust in nuclear engineering can be extended to trust in theoretical physics.
>
> (111)

So, relying on identifiable experts in neighboring domains can help us identify experts in murkier domains.

3 Credentials

Credentials also offer cues to expertise.[14] You are better off trusting a board-certified heart surgeon than an individual who claims expertise but lacks these same credentials. Degrees, awards, publications, and certifications can all indicate expertise or at least that the individual in question is in an improved epistemic position.

4 Reputation

Along these same lines, the reputation of a putative expert within their domain of inquiry can indicate their expertise. Consensus amongst those in the field can show that the individual in question is seen to be well-positioned to answer such questions. Other individuals in the field can determine the quantity and quality of evidence possessed as well as the individual's ability to assess that evidence.[15]

Of course, the question 'who are the relevant experts?' is itself a question that you can inquire about. And, typically, this question too will be outside of your area of expertise. So, given the conclusion of this chapter, it is a question that you are better off outsourcing to the relevant experts – the experts about expertise. There are people who have thought long and hard about expertise and are more likely to be able to determine who the relevant experts are than anyone who has not done so. So, this too is a question that we can reasonably outsource to more capable parties.

Of course, none of these indicators of expertise are guarantees. We can still get it wrong. Reasonable deference may still be hard in many cases.[16] The claim here is only that the problem of expert identification is not inherently insurmountable. We do have some tools at our disposal. It is also important to remember that all we are after here is someone who is in a significantly better epistemic position on the matter. We don't need to be able to distinguish who among the top ten leading economists is in fact the very best. All that is needed is to find someone who is significantly better than we are. This is a much more modest goal. As Hardwig (1985) puts it:

> generally I can find someone whose opinion is more informed than mine and who can refer me to someone who is knowledgeable about whether or not p. And even if a layman, because of his relative inability to discriminate among experts, ends up appealing to a lesser instead of a greater expert, the lesser expert's opinion will still be better than the layman's.

(341)

OK, third and final response to the initial worry. The difficulty in determining the relevant experts is only a reason to think for ourselves instead, if our prospects for individual inquiry regarding the target question are better than our prospects at determining who the relevant experts are. For instance, if I'm wondering whether tax cuts boost the economy, I can either i) try to answer that question for myself, or ii) try and figure out who the relevant experts are. Given that I am not an expert in the domain in which my question resides, the prospects of succeeding at the second task will typically be better than my prospects of succeeding at the first. This is so, even if it is still quite difficult to determine who the experts in the relevant domain are. Huemer (2005) agrees that it will typically be easier to answer questions about who the relevant experts are than it will be for a layperson to answer questions in their area of expertise. For instance, he notes that in legal trials, experts are called on to testify to matters of their expertise (forensic experts, medical experts, financial experts, etc.), but we don't typically call on experts to testify to who the relevant experts are. This is some indication that we are better at doing that task, or at least that we take ourselves to be. If this is right, then with the goal of determining the answer to my question, I will often be better off trying to determine who the experts are than in trying to answer the target question myself, even if identifying the experts isn't an easy task.

So, while identifying the experts is not always easy, and while it is something that we can get wrong, this worry is not sufficient to stall our project.

THE UPSHOT

What the argument from expertise shows us is that for nearly any question you may want to investigate, there is someone else who is better suited to the task. For such questions, someone else is in a better epistemic position on the matter, and thus, more likely than you are to uncover the truth. Further, given that you are not yourself an expert about such matters, adding your own individual inquiry into the mix will not significantly improve your likelihood as successful inquiry. In fact, it is plausible that supplementing the expert opinion with your own research will only serve to lessen your odds of success. Given all of this, thinking for yourself is typically unnecessary. So, it is often OK not to think for yourself.

In the next chapter, we will supplement the argument from expertise with the argument from evidential swamping. Whereas the argument from expertise was concerned with individual experts, the argument from evidential swamping is concerned with the state of a given debate in the relevant field of expertise. While the motivating considerations are distinct, the conclusion of this argument too is that it is often unnecessary to think for yourself.

The Argument from Evidential Swamping

3

In this chapter we will examine the second argument that thinking for yourself is unnecessary, and thus, that it is fine not to do so. The first argument, the argument from expertise, claimed that for nearly any question you want to answer, there is someone else who is better positioned to answer that question. Given this, and your desire to determine the answer, you are better off deferring to that individual. This makes thinking for yourself about the issue unnecessary. This second argument, the argument from evidential swamping, builds on the first. However, rather than looking to individual experts, this argument focuses on the state of the debate amongst the relevant experts in a field as a whole. In brief, the claim is that what you should believe about a matter is determined by the state of expert opinion on that matter. Since that is so, thinking for yourself on the matter (as a non-expert) will not change what it is rational for you to believe about the issue. However, if thinking for yourself won't change what it is rational for you to believe, then thinking for yourself is unnecessary. In other words, it is OK not to think for yourself.

Here is the rough idea. Our evidence about what the relevant experts believe about some matter is so strong that it will swamp, or entirely outweigh, any evidence that we (as novices) gather or evaluate on our own. Since the experts have superior bodies of evidence, and they are superior at evaluating that

DOI: 10.4324/9781003369004-4

evidence, and they are many whereas any of us are just one, our own intellectual contributions to any debate will be too insignificant to shift what it is reasonable for us to believe. Our own intellectual efforts are like a few grains of sand which don't make much of a contribution when compared to the beach of expertise.

We can put the argument from evidential swamping as follows:

1. What you should believe about a matter is entirely determined by the state of expert opinion on that matter.[1]
2. If so, then your non-expert individual inquiry will not change what you should believe about a matter.
3. If your non-expert individual inquiry will not change what you should believe about a matter, then your non-expert individual inquiry is unnecessary.
4. So, your non-expert individual inquiry is unnecessary.

MOTIVATING THE ARGUMENT

Let's unpack things by looking at each premise of the argument in turn.

Why think (1) is true? Ask yourself the following questions. What should you believe about the number of moons that Jupiter has? What should you believe about the effects of dropping the interest rate? What should you believe about the life expectancy of squirrels? What should you believe about the dates of the King Henry VIII's rule? In each of these cases, you should believe in line with what the relevant experts believe. If you, as a non-expert, come to a belief that conflicts with what the experts think, then your belief is not reasonable. You should revise it. After all, the experts are those who are most likely to be correct about matters in their domain of expertise. If anyone is going to get it right, it is the experts.

We quickly confront an issue here. The experts don't always agree. Regarding the existence of climate change, around 97% of climate scientists agree that it is occurring and caused by humans.[2] Regarding the benefits of flossing your teeth, the advertisements typically say something like "nine out ten dentists agree." While there is overwhelming agreement amongst the relevant experts regarding both of these claims, neither is unanimous. In fact, unanimity on any interesting issue is quite rare, at least once we get a significant number of people involved. That said, it would be misleading at best to say that climate change and the effectiveness of flossing are controversial. So, it will be helpful to distinguish several different ways that expert opinion can be distributed. The 'state of the debate' amongst the relevant experts regarding some proposition, p, can be in one of the following states:

> *State of Full Consensus*: Every relevant expert agrees about p.
> *State of Partial Consensus*: Full consensus is not achieved, but there is a clear dominant view amongst the relevant experts regarding p.
> *State of Disarray*: The opinions of the relevant experts are sufficiently dispersed, so as to prevent either full or partial consensus regarding p.[3]

With these distinctions in hand, we can see that the issues of both climate change and the benefits of flossing enjoy a state of partial consensus amongst the relevant experts. While there is not unanimous agreement, there is a clear dominant view amongst the relevant experts. In cases like this, where there is a clear dominant view amongst the experts, the rational thing for us to believe is that dominant view. The best explanation as to why 97% of climate scientists believe that the climate is changing is that the climate is indeed changing. The best explanation of why nine out of ten dentists believe that flossing is beneficial for one's dental health is that it is. Expert agreement is a powerful reason to believe in line with the experts.

So, for instance, you should believe that climate change is happening, and you should believe that flossing improves your dental health. You should believe these things because of the overwhelming agreement amongst the relevant experts. The state of partial consensus amongst the relevant experts makes these things rational for you to believe. For similar reasons, you should believe that Jupiter has 79 moons and that squirrels on average live for about seven years (in case you were wondering).

Of course, there isn't always a clear dominant view amongst the relevant experts. Some issues are quite contentious. When it comes to questions like whether God exists, whether there should be open borders, whether humans have free will, or whether there should be a meat tax, there is no dominant view amongst the relevant experts.[4] On matters like these, and many more, expert opinion is sufficiently dispersed amongst the various options. There is no clear dominant expert view. However, in these cases too, what we should believe about the matter is still determined by the state of the debate amongst the experts. When expert opinion is in a state of disarray, there is no dominant view to defer to, nevertheless, what we should believe about the issue is determined by what the experts believe.

In cases where expert opinion is in a state of disarray, we should suspend judgment about the matter. We suspend judgment about a proposition when we don't believe it (conclude that it is true) nor do we disbelieve it (conclude that it is false). In suspending judgment, we make no conclusion about whether the proposition is true or false (even though we know it is one or the other). So, why suspend? Well, if those who are best positioned to determine the answer to our question have been unable to collectively do so, then this precludes us from having a rational belief on the matter. In other words, the state of expert disagreement undermines the rationality of any position we may take on the matter besides suspending judgment.[5]

When expert opinion is in a state of disarray, we have good reason to believe that our evidence is not good enough, or the interpretation of it is too contentious. Either way, our grounds for belief are inadequate to support a positive belief on the matter.

So, regarding God's existence, whether people have free will, and whether there should be open borders, the rational thing for you to do is suspend judgment. Given the widespread disagreement amongst the relevant experts, this is the only rational response for you to have. Since those who are most likely to determine the answer have been unable to collectively do so, suspending judgment is called for.

So much for premise (1). What about premise (2)? Why think that these considerations have it that non-expert individual inquiry won't change what it is rational for you to believe? Here it is helpful to consider our two types of cases separately. Let's start with the easy case, when there is consensus (partial or full) amongst the relevant experts. Let's use our climate change example. You know that 97% of climate scientists believe that climate change is real, but suppose that you still want to look into it for yourself. You want to do your own research and think for yourself. You are perfectly within your rights to do so. How might that inquiry go? Suppose you collect significant amounts of the relevant direct evidence, and you conclude that climate change is happening. OK. That's reasonable for you to conclude, but it is no more reasonable for you to believe this now than it was when you believed this solely on the basis of the expert testimony. You already had excellent reasons to believe this. Your individual inquiry did not significantly improve things. After all, you are just a novice in this area.

To help see this, let's extrapolate yourself away from the situation. You still know that 97% of climate scientists believe that climate change is real, but then you learn that this individual, Novice Norman, has also been looking into the issue. He has investigated the issue, and he has also concluded that climate change is real. Wow, what a real game changer! Has your epistemic standpoint on the issue improved since learning about Norman's novice investigation? Of course not! And the same holds for Norman himself. His individual inquiry did not change what he is reasonable in believing nor did it change how reasonable he is in believing it. Neither his belief, nor your belief, that climate change is real is now better supported after this novice inquiry has been conducted. Any evidence he gathers does nothing to add to the weighty reasons that come from expert consensus.

OK, but your, or Norman's, individual inquiry could have gone differently. Suppose having acquired the relevant direct evidence and given it your best evaluation, you come away with no idea about what the climate science evidence supports. After all, you are not a climate scientist, and evaluating lots of the relevant evidence takes significant background knowledge and skills that you probably don't possess (I don't either). So, you come away from your inquiry thinking that you should suspend judgment – neither concluding that climate change is true, nor concluding that it is false – you are unable to make heads or tails of the debate. Now, after your failed individual inquiry, what should you believe about climate change? You should still believe it is happening, of course! After all, you know that 97% of climate scientists have evaluated the relevant evidence that way, and unlike you, they do have the requisite knowledge and skills to make those evaluations. So, in cases where you can't make heads or tails of what the evidence supports, you are left where you began – you should still believe in line with the consensus expert view. Your inability to see it for yourself makes you no less reasonable in believing that climate change is happening. Again, this is due to the overwhelming evidential power of expert consensus.

A final option is that you engage in your own inquiry, you do your own research, and come to the conclusion that climate change is not occurring; you come to a different conclusion than the expert consensus. Having acquired the relevant direct evidence, and given it your best evaluation, you take it to support the denial of climate change. Alright. Now having done so, what is it reasonable for you to believe about climate change? Here too, you should still believe that climate change is occurring. After all, you still know that 97% of climate scientists believe that. While that's not the way that you saw it, climate scientists are in a far better epistemic position to answer this question. The odds that you got it right, while 97% of climate scientists all got it wrong, are astronomically small. In other words, it is not reasonable for you to believe that you, as a novice, got it right, while the vast majority of the experts all got it wrong. So, here too, the reasonable thing for you to believe is that climate change is happening. Thinking for yourself didn't change that.

What this goes to show is that no matter how your own individual novice inquiry goes, what you are justified in believing about climate change does not change. In each scenario, you should believe in line with expert consensus, regardless of the outcome of thinking for yourself, and regardless of the result of your own individual inquiry. The same goes for any other issue that enjoys expert consensus.

So much for the easy case. What about cases where the state of expert opinion is in disarray? Don't such cases leave more room for thinking for yourself? After all, a natural thought is that if the experts can't figure it out, then it is up to you to inquire and make your own determination about what the answer is. We might be tempted to think that in such cases it is everyone for themselves. We want answers to our questions, and so if there is no unified answer to get from the experts, doesn't that license us each to figure out our own answer, to make our own determination about what to believe?

In short, no. Again, if you want to think about such questions, that is perfectly fine. You are free to look at the evidence and make of it what you will, but you won't thereby be reasonable in believing the conclusion that you happen to come to. Why not? By stipulation, you are not an expert in the relevant field. Others are. Others have a much more extensive body of relevant evidence than you have, or will acquire, are more adept at evaluating that evidence, and have spent much more time dedicated to doing so. Given all of this, if they (the relevant experts) cannot come to a unified, settled view on the matter, you have strong reason to doubt any conclusion that you may come to. If the experts cannot collectively figure this problem out, then you shouldn't think that you (as a novice) did.

Here's an example to help motivate the point. When I teach philosophy classes, I want students to think for themselves about the complex topics that we discuss.[6] I expose them to central readings, arguments, and objections, and I want them to wrestle with them and make their own evaluation of things. For instance, we might be discussing the nature of free will. We look at readings and arguments on a number of different positions on the issue: arguments for compatibilism, incompatibilism, free will skepticism, and so forth. Sometimes, a student will approach me after such a section and say something like "I've figured it out! Now I know what the nature of free will is." I don't usually say something quite this blunt, but I typically think to myself, "No, you haven't." After all, this student has been thinking about free will for a handful of weeks, and has been doing so with a mind that is still developing, and has only been exposed to a small fraction of the literature. At the same time, this is an issue that our greatest minds have been wrestling with for years upon years and been unable to agree about. If those who are in the best position to find the answer have been unable to collectively do so, what are the odds that this student has done so in just a couple of weeks? While it is not impossible, it isn't a reasonable bet. In other words, the student should not think that they have found the answer, even if one of the answers strikes them as correct or even obvious. The widespread disagreement amongst the relevant experts is such powerful evidence that it swamps whatever reasons they may have gained to believe their favored view.[7]

On to premise (3). Why does this render novice individual inquiry unnecessary? Well, let's return to the point of inquiry. We inquire to determine the answer to our question. If what it is reasonable for us to believe about the answer will not change from conducting our own individual inquiry, our own individual inquiry is intellectually superfluous. Let's first think about other factors that won't change what it is reasonable for you to believe. When it comes to what it is reasonable to believe, what matters is the relevant evidence and what it supports. It doesn't matter who your favorite band is, what you had for breakfast, or what clothes you are wearing. So long as those things don't affect your evidence, they are irrelevant to what it is reasonable for you to believe. Since they are evidentially irrelevant, there are no intellectual requirements regarding these things. You don't need to have a certain favorite band, have had a certain breakfast, or be wearing certain clothes to form a rational belief. Since none of these things affect what it is reasonable for you to believe, or how reasonable you are in believing it, there are no intellectual requirements concerning them. As we have seen, thinking about things for yourself also won't change *what* answer it is reasonable for you to believe (if any), and it won't change *how* reasonable it is for you to believe that answer. The balance of our reasons for regarding the question at hand will remain roughly the same after individual novice inquiry as it was before, since any reasons we gain will be swamped by the powerful evidence regarding the state of the debate.

So, premises (1)–(3) are all pretty plausible. Further, if they are all true, then it follows that non-expert inquiry is unnecessary. Given that thinking for yourself often won't change what you should believe, it is often unnecessary. As we saw in the previous chapter, for almost any question you want to answer, you will not be an expert. For each of us, our expertise is quite limited. It follows that for most questions that we want to answer, our own inquiry will be unnecessary. Alternatively put, for almost every question you confront, it is perfectly fine not to think about it for yourself. What you should believe (if anything) is already set by the state of expert opinion.[8]

Having made a second theoretical case that thinking for your-self is often unnecessary, let's again look at how these consid-erations apply to cases in order to gain further support for our conclusion.

> QUANTUM: Jamal recently watched a video on the two-slit experiment. The video opened his eyes up to the mysteries of the quantum world. After doing some further research, Jamal becomes familiar with the leading interpretations of quantum mechanics. He also becomes aware of the wide-spread disagreement amongst leading physicists as to which interpretation is correct. Jamal really wants to understand the quantum world, but given that the leading physicists can't come to any kind of consensus, it is extraordinarily unlikely that Jamal's own inquiry into the matter will con-clude with him figuring it out. He concludes that he should suspend judgment.

Jamal is correctly responding to his evidence. The evidence of widespread expert disagreement is powerful evidence. Suspending judgment is the appropriate attitude for Jamal to take. In this case, Jamal sees that his own individual inquiry is not going to change what it is rational for him to believe, so he opts not to think for himself about the issue. This decision is perfectly fine. After all, his own individual inquiry will not change what it is rational for him to believe about the quan-tum world.

> ALGEBRA: Ankita is in college algebra. She's doing well in the course, but it takes effort. One night she is working on some problems. Her algebra book has the answers to the problems in the back of the book, so students can check

their work. After working on problem 7(b), Ankita looks to the back of the book. The back of the book states that the answer to 7(b) is 13. When Ankita did the problem herself, she came to the conclusion that the answer was 17. While textbooks do sometimes contain misprints, the rational thing for Ankita to believe is that the answer is 13, and that she has made an error in her calculations.

In this case, Ankita has undergone individual inquiry. She thought about the problem for herself before consulting the expert opinion. Perhaps, if she had a good track record at completing such problems, she was even rational in believing that the answer was 17 *before* she checked the back of the book. However, once she learns what the expert opinion is on the matter, she is not rational to stick to her conclusion. The best explanation of this state of affairs is that Ankita has made an error in her calculations.

> RECYCLING: Kristie recently read an op-ed advocating for libertarianism and the privatization of recycling measures. The author's case sounds quite plausible to her, and after thinking it over for a while she becomes convinced that privatization is the way to go here. However, Kristie also knows, by way of the article, that this conclusion is quite contentious amongst the relevant experts. She can't see why. The case, to her, seems clear and compelling, so she confidently concludes that privatization is the way to go.

Despite her confidence, Kristie's conclusion is not reasonable. It is not supported by her total evidence, since she knows about the extensive expert disagreement on the issue. After all, she is aware that those disagreeing experts have better evidence, are better qualified to evaluate that evidence, and have been thinking far more extensively about the issue than she has. It would be hubris on her part to think that she figured out the issue while the experts have collectively been unable to do so.

LEARNING STYLES: Brantley is studying to become an elementary school teacher. He has always believed that it is important for teachers to cater to their students' different learning styles. In his psychology class, Brantley comes to find out that the idea that students learn better when taught in line with their preferences is widely considered a myth amongst the relevant experts. When subjected to tests, the data simply do not bear this out. Nevertheless, the claim still strikes Brantley as obvious. Seeing the findings of the studies to the contrary doesn't move him. He is unconvinced. Of course, Brantley thinks, students learn better in their preferred learning style.

Brantley has a strong impression that he is correct. But, strong impressions can still be mistaken. Further, when those strong impressions conflict with the expert consensus, there is very good reason to think that they are in fact mistaken. Brantley's own evaluation of the data is but one small piece of the evidential pile. The far weightier evidence consists of the expert opinions that stand in widespread agreement on the issue.

LINCOLN: Haya recently watched a documentary on the US civil war. In it, she heard several historians report that Lincoln had proposed sending freed slaves to Central America in a policy called 'colonization'. This fact struck Haya as surprising and inspired her to do a little digging of her own. After spending some time looking at a couple of other sources on the matter, she came to the same conclusion, that this often-unreported claim is true.

In this case, Haya's individual inquiry results in the same answer as the experts. Her inquiry didn't hurt her or lead her away from the truth, but at the same time, it wasn't necessary either. After thinking for herself, Haya is left to believe the same thing that she was rational in believing before her individual inquiry, and she is no more reasonable in believing it. Adding her novice assessment of the evidence to the total evidence is far too insignificant to change what that evidence supports or the degree to which it supports it.

What is the moral to draw from these cases? In each of these cases we see that individual inquiry didn't change things, rationally speaking. In each case, what our subject was rational in believing didn't change, and their support for believing it didn't change either. Given this, their individual inquiry was simply unnecessary. It may have been a fine thing to do, but it wasn't rationally required, it was superfluous. And it is OK not to do things that are not necessary.

THE UPSHOT

Let's take stock, having examined our two central arguments: the argument from expertise and the argument from evidential swamping. What we've seen so far is that for nearly any question you want to investigate as a non-expert: i) there is someone better positioned to answer your question, and ii) conducting your own individual inquiry will not change what you are reasonable in believing about the answer. So, with the goal of determining the answer to your question, you should defer to someone who is more likely to be able to answer it. You should rely on your more capable epistemic surrogates. In the very least, you are not required to think for yourself. Further, given the evidential power of expert opinion, also thinking about things for yourself will not change what you should believe, and it won't change how reasonable you are in believing it. If the experts agree, you should believe in line with the experts, and adding your novice 2-cents to the mix won't change the reasonability of that belief. If the expert opinion is in disarray, then a rational belief on the matter simply isn't up for grabs. If those most likely to answer the question haven't been able to come to anything like a consensus, then adding your own novice inquiry to the mix won't resolve the issue. The only rational thing to do in such a situation is to withhold judgment and wait for things to improve. What all of this shows is that thinking for yourself, when you are not yourself an expert, is unnecessary, and it is perfectly fine to not do things that are unnecessary. Again, if you want to look into the matter for yourself, you are free to do so, but given that what you are rational in believing will not change, it is perfectly fine not to do so as well. It is OK not to think for yourself.

At this point you might be wondering why the arguments considered thus far don't support a stronger conclusion – that you *shouldn't* think for yourself. After all, if thinking for yourself isn't going to change what it is rational to believe, isn't thinking for yourself minimally a waste of time, and perhaps even more damaging than that? While I do think the arguments discussed thus far do show that thinking for yourself is overrated, I also think that there are reasons to not abandon it as well. First, recall that our arguments were restricted to cases where you are not yourself an expert. Sometimes you are an expert, and when you are, it is important to think for yourself.[9] While the range of anyone's expertise is limited, there will typically be questions that we are each at least as well positioned to answer as anyone else. Second, we will see reasons in the rest of the book to think for yourself, even as a non-expert. I don't want to spoil things here, but Chapters 6, 8, and 9 all look at reasons why thinking for yourself can be beneficial. In each case I argue that these reasons don't *require* us to think for ourselves, but they do show why the stronger conclusion, that we should not think for ourselves, is too strong.

This concludes the positive argument for this central conclusion of the book. In what remains we will examine a series of objections, each of which claims that something has gone wrong in the path to this conclusion. Spoiler alert: the objections all fail. However, if you want to think about them for yourself, you are encouraged to read on.

4

Having made the case that thinking for yourself is unnecessary, the rest of the book motivates and responds to a number of pressing objections to this central conclusion. In this chapter, we will explore the objection that in not thinking for yourself, you fail to be an epistemically autonomous agent. In particular, the worry here is that being epistemically autonomous is of great intellectual importance, and the epistemically autonomous person does not outsource most of their intellectual projects. If a significant amount of thinking for yourself is essential to epistemic autonomy, and epistemic autonomy is quite valuable, then we have a powerful reason to think for ourselves. In other words, the objection claims that it is not OK to forego epistemic autonomy, and that is precisely what someone who does not think for themselves does. In response, I'll argue that this objection conflates epistemic autonomy with intellectual individualism, and this is a mistake. This is a mistake, in part, because the idea of intellectual individualism is a myth. No one can do it on their own. I'll also distinguish several senses of epistemic autonomy that are each valuable and important, and I'll then show that neither kind of autonomy conflicts with our central conclusion.

DOI: 10.4324/9781003369004-5

Let's start by thinking about autonomy more generally. As political philosopher Joseph Raz (1988: 407) has put it, the autonomous person determines the course of their life for themselves. Along these lines, it is common to see autonomy as a kind of self-governance or self-direction. Autonomous people are able to live their lives as they see fit. They are free from certain kinds of interference with their goals like coercion and manipulation. Autonomous people are guided by their own goals, desires, and values; they live authentic lives. Given this, it is easy to see why autonomy has been seen as a central moral and political value.[1] The individual who lacks autonomy is not free, they do not determine their own life, and this is a great loss. Take, for instance, the example of an oppressed people group. Oppressed people are not autonomous. Their lives are guided by external forces that they neither endorse nor embrace, and they are thereby unable to direct the course of their own lives. The value of autonomy shows us at least part of what is wrong with oppression.

In *On Liberty*, Mill gives stresses the value of autonomy as follows:

> A person whose desires and impulses are his own – are the expression of his own nature, as it has been developed and modified by his own culture – is said to have a character. One whose desires and impulses are not his own has no character, no more than a steam engine has a character.
>
> (Mill 1956/1859: 73)

Here, autonomy is seen as central to living any kind of life at all. Autonomy is also a central value in Kantian moral philosophy. According to Kant, autonomy is the foundational principle of all of morality. Autonomy is the basis for which we owe ourselves, and others, moral respect. In addition, autonomy has also been seen as a kind of freedom, and as such, it has often been linked to a strong kind of individualism.[2] We will return to this connection shortly.

So much for autonomy more generally, what about epistemic autonomy in particular?[3] Epistemic autonomy is autonomy in the intellectual realm. So, epistemically autonomous agents direct the course of their intellectual lives, they are self-directed, authentic thinkers. Epistemically autonomous individuals are free from manipulation and coercion in their intellectual pursuits. Just like moral autonomy is seen as central to moral agency, and political autonomy necessary for political agency, epistemic autonomy is often seen as essential to epistemic agency.

However, several philosophers have seen a conflict between deference and epistemic autonomy.[4] For instance, Fricker (2006a) claims that an epistemically autonomous person "takes no one else's word for anything but accepts only what she has found out for herself, relying only on her own cognitive faculties and investigative inferential powers." (225) Similarly, Zagzebski (2007) identifies the autonomous thinker as someone who, when they find out that another believes some proposition, "will demand proof of [that proposition] that she can determine by the use of her own faculties, given her own previous beliefs, but she will never believe anything on testimony." (252)

Thomas Scanlon (1972) also sees a conflict between autonomous thinking and deference in claiming the following:

> [A]n autonomous person cannot accept without independent consideration the judgment of others as to what

he should believe or what he should do. He may rely on the judgment of others, but when he does so he must be prepared to advance independent reasons for thinking their judgment likely to be correct, and to weigh the evidential value of their opinion against contrary evidence.

(216)

While Hardwig (1985) is fully on board with the central conclusion of this book, he too thought that such an intellectual reliance on others conflicted with epistemic autonomy. Here is how he put it:

If I am correct, appeals to epistemic authority are essentially ingredient in much of our knowledge. Appeals to the authority of experts often provide justification for claims to know, as well as grounding rational belief. At the same time, however, the epistemic superiority of the expert to the layman implies rational authority over the layman, undermining the intellectual autonomy of the individual and forcing a reexamination of our notion of rationality.

(336)

So, while Hardwig thinks that novices should rely on experts to answer their questions, he nevertheless sees such a reliance as being in tension with epistemic autonomy.[5] If deference and epistemic autonomy are in conflict, and epistemic autonomy is of great value, then it looks like there is something wrong with deference, even deference to the experts. If such deference comes at the cost of our autonomy, isn't there something wrong with it? Aren't we then required to think for ourselves? According to the autonomy objection this is precisely the case. There is a requirement to think for yourself because your epistemic autonomy requires that you think for yourself, and like your moral and political autonomy, your epistemic autonomy is not something to be sacrificed.

While there is a good deal of intuitive pull to the autonomy objection, I think that it fails. Considerations of epistemic autonomy do not show that we are required to think for ourselves. To see this, we need to first distinguish epistemic autonomy from intellectual individualism.

THE MYTH OF INTELLECTUAL INDIVIDUALISM

It can be tempting to equate epistemic autonomy with a kind of rugged intellectual individualism. On such a picture the intellectually autonomous individual is self-reliant and does not depend on anyone else in their inquiry. According to this view, autonomous thinkers insist on figuring everything out for themselves. Those philosophers who saw a conflict between epistemic autonomy and deference all thought of epistemic autonomy as a kind of intellectual individualism. For instance, Hardwig (1985) also claimed the following:

> But if I were to pursue epistemic autonomy across the board, I would succeed only in holding relatively uninformed, unreliable, crude, untested, and therefore irrational beliefs. If I would be rational, I can never avoid some epistemic dependence on experts, owing to the fact that I believe more than I can become fully informed about.
>
> (340)

So, Hardwig identifies epistemic autonomy with a kind of intellectual individualism, and concludes that we are better off without both. We need to rely on the experts. While he was right to abandon intellectual individualism, I will argue that it was a mistake to confuse intellectual individualism with epistemic autonomy. Before turning to what epistemic autonomy is, however, let's see why it is not this kind of rugged intellectual individualism.

The picture of autonomy as individualism casts the hermit as the ideal. The hermit doesn't rely on anyone else for anything. They are entirely self-dependent and self-reliant. However, few of us aspire to such of life of seclusion, whether intellectual or otherwise, nor do we see it as an ideal. We don't see the hermit's life as less oppressed or more authentic than our own. So, perhaps there's more to autonomy.

The picture of epistemic autonomy as intellectual individualism simply doesn't fit the kind of creatures that we are.[6] We are social creatures. If our intellectual lives were lived in isolation, they would be nasty, brutish, and short. Given our finite time and limited cognitive resources, without relying on others there is very little that we could come to understand about the world. Hardwig was right about that. Left to our own intellectual devices, the scope of our beliefs would be incredibly narrow and the support for our beliefs would be exceedingly flimsy. If in doubt, take a moment to think about what things you have figured out for yourself, all on your own, without the help of others. The intellectually independent life is not an intellectually healthy life.

This fact is further revealed in contemporary scientific practice. Scientific research is not an individual activity. Large groups of scientists work together on complex projects and are often spread across countries and even continents. In fact, one recent physics paper lists over 5,000 authors![7] Much of this research simply could not be done by any one individual. Such research requires too many sets of specialized skills and too much diverse knowledge. It is too much for any one individual, never mind the fact that no one individual could have the time to conduct all of the relevant data. However, the group nature of such scientific research is not a drawback, or an infringement on the autonomy of its researchers, it's an asset. We can do more, and we can do better, when we work together. This is not unique to scientific inquiry either, the same is true of inquiry more broadly. As they say, it takes a village.

So, what does all of this mean for epistemic autonomy and thinking for yourself? We need to distinguish epistemic autonomy from the rugged intellectual individualism discussed earlier. There are two important respects in which autonomous thinking is actually a group project itself, and not something that is simply done on your own.[8] That's right, thinking for yourself isn't even something you can do for yourself. Let's see why even in thinking for ourselves we are depending on others.

First, we wouldn't even be equipped to think for ourselves if it wasn't for others. This point is pretty obvious, if we stop and think about it. We rely on others for both the tools that we use in thinking as well as the development of the needed intellectual skills to use those tools well. Developing our epistemic autonomy requires relying on others for language, ideas, information, and all kinds of other intellectual goods. Similarly, sharpening our critical thinking skills is also best done together, not alone. So, rather than being in conflict with our autonomy, a healthy reliance on others is actually required for its development. We couldn't even be intellectually autonomous if it wasn't for others. As Baier (1985) puts it, "A person, perhaps, is best seen as one who was long enough dependent upon other persons to acquire the essential arts of personhood. Persons essentially are second persons, who grow up with other persons." (84)

We all owe a debt of gratitude to our intellectual communities. OK, so that's one sense in which our epistemic autonomy depends on others. You might think that it doesn't really count. Of course, we need other people to even exist, but once we do, you might think the autonomous person says, "I'll take it from here." However, our dependence on others in being epistemically autonomous extends beyond the mere development of our rational capacities.

A second way in which we rely on others is in the very exercising of our epistemic autonomy. We think for ourselves well when we think with others. Thinking for yourself well requires you to think about other perspectives, both real and imagined. You need to see yourself as answerable to others for your views, and as having reasons that you could give to others as to why you believe what you do.[9] Westlund (2012) makes this same point claiming, "the autonomous agent has a disposition to hold herself answerable, for elements of her motivational hierarchy, in the face of critical challenges posed by others." (65–6) To be rational, we need to see ourselves as accountable to others for our own thinking – for why we came to the conclusions that we did. As King (2021: 88) nicely puts it, autonomy requires thinking *for* yourself, not thinking *by* yourself. So, both the development and the utilization of our epistemic autonomy is interpersonal and relational, not individualistic. Thinking for yourself is something that we do together.

This is a relational conception of autonomy, one that appreciates our social nature and deep dependence on others.[10] The idea of relational autonomy developed out of the work of feminist philosophers who were critiquing the pervasive conception of autonomy as self-reliance. As Mackenzie and Stoljar (2000) describe it, relational autonomy is, "premised on a shared conviction that persons are socially embedded, that agents' identities are formed within the context of social relationships and shaped by a complex of intersecting social determinants, such as race, class, gender, and ethnicity." (4) Understood as relational autonomy, autonomy conflicts with heteronomy, not with dependence.[11] The heteronomous individual is one who is subject to the rule or power of another. Heteronomy is domination, not dependence. As Elgin (2013) describes the difference: an autonomous agent is one who "makes the laws that bind her," whereas a heteronomous subject "is bound by constraints that he neither makes nor endorses." (140) So, it is not dependence that conflicts with autonomy.

Intellectual individualism is simply a myth. It is a "perversion of autonomy,"[12] one that is unobtainable for creatures like us, and we have good reason not to want it anyway. We can do better with regard to our intellectual goals by relying on others.[13]

Why does all of this matter? Epistemic autonomy has often been understood as requiring you to do it all yourself, to do your own research, to not just listen to the experts. Understood as relational autonomy, however, epistemic autonomy has no such individualistic implications. So understood, epistemic autonomy is perfectly compatible with listening to what others have to say, particularly those with the relevant expertise, and even deferring to them. The autonomous thinker needn't reinvent the intellectual wheel, so to speak; they are free to utilize the vast intellectual resources that are afforded to us by others. Just as the autonomous person does not need to grow all their own food, make all their own clothes, do all their own home repairs, and so forth, the epistemically autonomous individual does not need to do all their own inquiry either. We can learn from others, and rely on their expertise, even while being epistemically autonomous.

AUTONOMY AS INTELLECTUAL FREEDOM

If epistemic autonomy isn't intellectual individualism, then what is it? I actually doubt that there is any *one* thing that is epistemic autonomy. There are at least two senses of epistemic autonomy that are both important and valuable that I will explore here. Having laid out what they are, I will argue that neither one of them conflicts with our central conclusion.

Both of these conceptions of epistemic autonomy fit within Raz's broader idea that the autonomous person directs the course of their own lives. Epistemic autonomy, then, involves directing the course of one's intellectual life, but this can happen in importantly different respects. One sense of epistemic autonomy concerns a kind of intellectual freedom. Autonomous thinkers, in this sense, are free to think about what they want to, free to take on the intellectual projects of their choice, and they are not manipulated in their inquiry. This kind of epistemic autonomy consists in shaping the course of one's own intellectual life. Such autonomy rules out coercion, manipulation, and other ways of subjecting your intellectual will to another. A second, and distinct, sense of epistemic autonomy sees it as an intellectual virtue. In this sense, epistemically autonomous thinkers are good executive managers of their intellectual lives. As a character virtue, epistemic autonomy is a nurtured character trait of epistemic agents. This character trait is an intellectually good way to be, and consists of a conglomeration of cognitive dispositions, including having the proper motivation. So, we have epistemic autonomy as intellectual freedom and epistemic autonomy as an intellectual virtue. Let's further unpack each of these and see how neither sense of autonomy conflicts with deferring to others, and not thinking for yourself.

Let's start with epistemic autonomy as a kind of intellectual freedom. This first sense of epistemic autonomy is perhaps best captured in the work of C.A.J. Coady. According to Coady (2002), epistemic autonomy has three core components: independence, self-creation, and integrity. The first condition, independence, is a kind of negative freedom. An individual is independent when they have freedom from interference in their inquiry. We can see this as a kind of non-domination requirement for epistemic autonomy. Autonomous thinkers are not compelled to cognitively conform to the powers that be. Independent intellectual agents are free to develop mastery, or expertise, in the areas or ways that they see fit; they are free to think about what they want to think about and in the way that they want to think about it. Coady is clear that he is not thinking of independence as a kind of self-sufficiency (the kind we rejected earlier). Rather, independence here is simply a lack of forced compliance or conformity.

The second component of epistemic autonomy, self-creation, is freedom to create one's own distinctive intellectual life. So, autonomous thinkers order their intellectual lives in ways that they see fit; they are the authors of their intellectual lives. (365–6) This component of epistemic autonomy consists of prioritizing one's intellectual projects in ways that align with one's values and interests. In doing so, autonomous thinkers shape their intellectual lives in distinctive ways. Finally, in addition to the negative freedom of independence, and the positive freedom of self-creation, Coady posits the third component of epistemic autonomy, integrity. According to Coady (2002), integrity amounts to standing up for truth, even in circumstances where doing so will result in negative consequences. (363) So understood, integrity amounts to a kind of intellectual courage, where one does not easily fold to external intellectual pressures. While this third component of Coady's account sounds more like an intellectual virtue, independence and self-creation each capture the idea of epistemic autonomy as a kind of right or intellectual freedom.

It is easy to see how there can be problematic violations of one's epistemic autonomy, understood as intellectual freedom. For instance, we can imagine a dictator, or a cult leader, that forbids people from asking certain questions, reading certain texts, or inquiring about certain matters. Such interference prevents individuals from living their intellectual lives as they see fit and it is clearly problematic.[14] We can also think of the student who wants to study philosophy, but their parents will only support them if they continue to pursue a degree in engineering. Such cases' interference with the intellectual pursuits of others is an interference with their autonomy and it is problematic because of that fact.[15]

However, not all intellectual interference may be problematic. One contemporary debate in epistemology concerns the permissibility of epistemic paternalism. Epistemic paternalism concerns interfering with the inquiry of someone else, without their consent, for their own epistemic good. Someone can interfere with the inquiry of another by either providing or withholding information from them. When this is done without their consent, and with their own intellectual best interest at heart, it is a case of epistemic paternalism. For instance, certain types of evidence are withheld from jurors, and arguments for young Earth creationism are withheld from science textbooks. In both cases, the relevant parties were not first consulted about the matter; they did not give their consent to have this information withheld. Further, in both cases this interference was done for their own good. Since jurors often incorrectly weigh certain types of evidence (e.g. past criminal records, withdrawn guilty pleas, testimonial hearsay, and so forth), they are more likely to get a correct verdict without seeing such evidence.[16] So, the interference is to help them reach the truth. Since hearing arguments for young Earth creationism will not help students form true beliefs about the origin of the Earth, such information is not helpful. So, in both of these cases, the idea is that certain information was withheld to better ensure that the individuals in question arrived at a true belief.[17]

One philosophical issue is whether acts of epistemic paternalism are justifiable.[18] Without entering too far into that debate here, it should be clear that acts of epistemic paternalism do conflict with agents' intellectual freedom. When individuals are given information they didn't ask for, or have information withheld from them without their consent, their intellectual pursuits are affected in ways that they did not agree to. In such situations, they are not governing their own intellectual lives. So, the debate about epistemic paternalism concerns whether it is permissible to infringe on individuals' epistemic autonomy, and whether the epistemic benefits of doing so outweigh the costs to their intellectual freedom. When an individual's inquiry is interfered with, their capacities for independence and self-creation (in Coady's sense) are affected.

While there is at least a tension between this sense of epistemic autonomy and epistemic paternalism, there is no such conflict between epistemic autonomy, so understood, and our central conclusion that it is OK not to think for yourself. On this picture of epistemic autonomy, autonomy is about intellectual self-direction, self-creation, and non-interference.

However, intellectual outsourcing, and extensive deference to others, is compatible with *all* of these things. One way that one can direct their own intellectual life is to direct it to defer to others who are better positioned to determine the answer. When no one is compelling this deference, such deference is not the result of any interference. Deference is a choice that comes from the agent themselves, it needn't be the result of coercion or manipulation. In fact, in can be precisely the way that one freely chooses to direct their own intellectual life.

Nguyen (2018b) argues that we can exhibit a kind of epistemic autonomy in deference, even when the expert's reasons are unclear to us:

> It is the capacity to invest others with intellectual trust, even when their intellectual work is not transparent to us. … I am autonomous because I have chosen and delegated responsibility to somebody out of an active sense of trust and because I treat myself as responsible for the whole.
>
> (116)

Nguyen calls this sense of autonomy 'delegational autonomy.'[19] Delegational autonomy is still a kind of autonomy since it still involves exercising control over one's intellectual life and directing its course. Along these same lines, Lillehammer (2014) claims that the example of Ulysses shows us that:

> [in] handing over the power of judgement to someone else in a particular situation I could be exercising self-governance at the level that really matters, if the case in question is one in which I correctly predict that I will be subject to moral or epistemic weakness in a particular situation.
>
> (119)

So, deference to the experts does not conflict with our intellectual freedom. Deference is just one more way that a subject can direct their intellectual lives. This meets Coady's independence condition. Further, when such deference concerns questions that the subject wants to have answered, such deference can even be a way of fulfilling self-creation. Deference can be one way in which an individual prioritizes various questions, values different answers, and expresses their intellectual interests. There is no conflict between deference and self-creation either.

So, not thinking for yourself does not compromise your epistemic autonomy as understood as a kind of intellectual freedom. If there is any conflict between not thinking for yourself and epistemic autonomy, it lies elsewhere.

AUTONOMY AS INTELLECTUAL VIRTUE

Let's now turn to epistemic autonomy as an intellectual virtue. To do so, we need to start by looking at what intellectual virtues are more generally. Intellectual virtues are the intellectual counterpart to moral virtues. In general, virtues are excellent character traits. Moral virtues are those character traits that make their possessor a morally good person. Some paradigm moral virtues are honesty, generosity, and courage. The generous person is disposed to act in a particular way across a wide variety of circumstances. Further, the generous person doesn't just give to other people, they do so for certain reasons, and with certain accompanying emotions. For instance, generous people don't give begrudgingly, and their primary motivation is not to get a tax break. Following Aristotle, virtues are often seen as a mean between two extremes of a given trait. To possess the virtue is to have the trait to the Goldilocks 'just right' amount. So, someone can be deficient or excessive in their generosity, but those with the virtue of generosity are generous to the right extent.

What about intellectual virtues? Paralleling moral virtues, intellectual virtues are cognitive character traits that make their possessor intellectually good.[20] Like moral virtues, intellectual virtues require being disposed to act in certain ways and to be accompanied by particular motivations.[21] Here, some paradigm examples are intellectual humility, intellectual perseverance, and open-mindedness. An intellectual virtue is a character trait of a good inquirer; they are traits that make an individual better-off epistemically. These character traits that help individuals in their intellectual pursuits of acquiring, maintaining, and distributing intellectual goods are like true beliefs or knowledge. Like with moral virtues, motives matter for intellectual virtues as well. Good intellectual character traits are motivated by a love of the truth. Jason Baehr (2011) sums things up nicely in claiming that intellectual virtue is "a character trait that contributes to its possessor's personal intellectual worth on account of its involving a positive psychological orientation toward epistemic goods." (102)

So much for intellectual virtues in general.[22] What about the virtue of epistemic autonomy in particular? Recently, more attention has been paid to the nature and value of the intellectual virtue of epistemic autonomy.[23] Many of these accounts connect this virtue to thinking for yourself in some way. To isolate the virtue here, let's start by thinking about how thinking for yourself can go wrong.[24] Consider the Maverick. The Maverick insists on seeing and figuring everything out for themself. They refuse to take anyone else's word for anything and ignores the intellectual resources of others.

This is an intellectually unhealthy life, one with an excess of thinking for yourself. On the other hand, we have the Codependent. The Codependent is too insecure to think about anything for themselves. They don't trust themselves with any intellectual projects because they are preoccupied with their own intellectual limitations. This too is an intellectually unhealthy life, one that exhibits a deficiency of thinking for yourself. Between these two intellectually unhealthy lives is the virtuous mean of epistemic autonomy – the virtue of thinking for yourself well.

For instance, according to Heather Battaly (2021), those who possess the trait of epistemic autonomy are disposed to think for themselves. Autonomous thinkers want to see it for themselves and rely on their own cognitive faculties and resources. This trait can be had to either an excess or to a deficiency. When had to an excess, individuals will think for themselves at the wrong times (e.g. when they are not reliable), in the wrong ways (e.g. using methods that are unreliable), or with respect to the wrong objects (e.g. intellectual projects that they are doomed to fail). (157) Individuals that exhibit a deficiency of epistemic autonomy fail to think for themselves when it is appropriate for them to do so. For instance, an individual may be reliable concerning a well-thought-out intellectual project, yet nevertheless defer to someone else less reliable.

Alongside the trait of epistemic autonomy, Battaly posits the trait of intellectual interdependence. The trait of intellectual interdependence concerns a disposition to think with others. Intellectually interdependent individuals consult others, collaborate with others, and rely on the intellectual resources of others. Intellectual interdependence too can be had to an excess or a deficiency. An excess of intellectual interdependence can result in uncritical deference and credulity. Individuals can also fail to think with others appropriately.

According to Battaly, the traits of epistemic autonomy and intellectual interdependence can each be intellectual virtues when possessed to the appropriate degree and coupled with the appropriate motivation for epistemic goods. So, the virtue of epistemic autonomy consists in a disposition to think for oneself *appropriately*. For Battaly, this includes a disposition to think for oneself at the right times, in the right ways, and with respect to the right objects, as well as a motivational disposition to do so because of a desire for epistemic goods. (164) The virtue of intellectual interdependence consists in a disposition to think with others appropriately. This includes a disposition to consistently think with others at the right times, in the right ways, and concerning the right objects, as well as a disposition to want to behave in those ways because of a desire for epistemic goods. (165)

Other epistemologists think of the virtue of epistemic autonomy as combining both of the traits referenced by Battaly. For instance, Nathan King (2021) sees the virtue of epistemic autonomy as thinking for yourself well *while relying appropriately on others*. (94) Exercising this virtue requires having the right object, using the right means, doing so on the right occasion, and with the right motivation. Thinking about the right object is important to our purposes. In determining whether you should think about a given topic for yourself, King councils that you ask whether it is wise for you to think independently about this topic given your background training and abilities. (95) King is also careful to emphasize that even when thinking independently, you need to be sensitive to expert opinion.

Along these same lines, I have elsewhere defended the following account of the intellectual virtue of epistemic autonomy:

The character virtue of [epistemic autonomy] characteristically involves the following dispositions:

(1) [cognitive] to make good judgments about how, and when, to rely on your own thinking, as well as how, and when, to rely on the thinking of others,
(2) [behavioral] to conduct inquiry in line with the judgments in (1), and
(3) [motivational] to do so because one loves the truth and appropriately cares about epistemic goods.

(Matheson 2021c: 182–3)

On this account, the virtue of epistemic autonomy has cognitive, behavioral, and motivational components. The cognitive component of epistemic autonomy consists of a disposition to make good judgments about when to think for oneself and when to rely more heavily on the thinking of others. Autonomous thinkers are discerning about how they should go about their inquiry, and they make good judgments about managing their inquiry. The behavioral component of epistemic autonomy consists in conducting their inquiry in accordance with those very judgments. So, epistemically autonomous thinkers also go about their inquiry in the way they see fit. Finally, the motivational component of epistemic autonomy has it that these judgments and activities are all fundamentally motivated by a love of truth and a desire for things of epistemic value. Thus, being epistemically autonomous requires making good judgments about how to balance relying on your own thinking with relying on the thinking of others, conducting inquiry according to those judgments, and so doing because of one's love of the truth.

What all of these accounts have in common is that epistemic autonomy is thought of as thinking for yourself well, or in the right way, and not just simply thinking for yourself. So, none of these accounts are committed to the myth of intellectual individualism. Further, each of these accounts of this intellectual virtue sees it as compatible with extensive deference to others.[25] In fact, appropriate deference to others is even a feature of this virtue. This is why epistemic autonomy can be considered a *social* intellectual virtue.[26]

While there might be disagreements concerning the scope of cases where thinking for yourself is appropriate,[27] each of these accounts acknowledges that the intellectual virtue is compatible with deference to others. One thought that should be avoided is that the mean of epistemic autonomy consists of thinking for yourself on roughly half of the occasions. While the language of 'mean' naturally suggests such a mid-way interpretation, it would be a mistake. For instance, the virtue of honesty can be seen as a mean between deficiency and excess. You can fail to tell the truth enough, and you can be brutally honest in sharing truths that just didn't need to be shared. While the virtue of honesty is a mean between these two extremes, this shouldn't be understood as implying that the virtue of honesty consists of telling the truth on approximately half of the occasions that present themselves. The virtue of honesty will require telling the truth in the vast majority of cases. So, just because a virtue falls between extremes of excess and deficiency, it doesn't follow that the virtue is somewhere close to the middle in terms of frequency. This matters for our purposes, because even while the intellectual virtue of epistemic autonomy requires finding the appropriate balance between thinking for yourself and depending on others, the appropriate balance need not look anything like a 50/50 proposition. It could be that the virtuous way to balance inquiry is with a very heavy reliance on others, just as the virtue of honesty will almost always call for telling the truth.

In fact, the accounts of the virtue of epistemic autonomy outlined here invite that very interpretation. For these authors, the cases that call for deference are those where the subject is unreliable or recognizes that others are much more reliable than themselves. However, these are precisely the types of cases that have been our concern – cases of novice inquiry. And as we have seen, most cases of inquiry are like this. So, rather than conflicting with this intellectual virtue, there is good reason that this intellectual virtue actually calls for people to not think for themselves in the types of cases that I have argued that it is OK not to think for yourself.

This leads to one last point. It is important to the intellectual virtue of epistemic autonomy that it is accompanied by the proper motivation – that the guiding motivation is a love of the truth and other epistemic goods. While deference can be done out of laziness or a desire to conform, the kind of deference that we have been concerned with is deference done in order to better achieve one's intellectual goals. It is a valuing of the truth that has motivated deference to the experts in the type of cases that we have been concerned with. So, even though intellectual virtues require a complex cognitive profile, none of the component parts conflict with deferring to those who are in a better epistemic position to determine the answer to your question. There is no conflict between extensive deference and the virtue of epistemic autonomy either.

THE UPSHOT

In this chapter we have examined the first of many objections to our central conclusion – that it is OK not to think for yourself. According to the autonomy objection, deference conflicts with epistemic autonomy, and epistemic autonomy is simply too valuable to be sacrificed. While a number of philosophers have been convinced that deference and autonomy conflict, this is due to confusing epistemic autonomy with intellectual individualism. As we have seen, intellectual individualism is a myth. There simply is no such thing. Autonomy is better understood relationally, in a way that appreciates our social dependence on others. With this confusion aside, we examined two senses of epistemic autonomy: autonomy as intellectual freedom and autonomy as an intellectual virtue. Having unpacked each sense of epistemic autonomy, we have seen that not only is there no conflict between either sense of autonomy and deference to the experts, but that there is even a deep coherence. One way to direct and determine your own intellectual life is to outsource your inquiry, and one way to show your love of truth is to rely on others who are better positioned to answer your questions than you are. So, there is no conflict between epistemic autonomy and not thinking for yourself on issues where you are a novice. But, this is just the first of many objections to consider. In the next chapter we will examine the objection that deferring to others amounts to a problematic kind of intellectual free-riding.

5

In this chapter we will examine the objection that failing to think for yourself amounts to a problematic kind of intellectual free-riding. Free-riding occurs when there is a common resource, and someone fails to contribute their fair share while nevertheless reaping the benefits. Individuals who don't think for themselves, yet rely on the thinking of others, gain the intellectual insights of others without making intellectual contributions of their own. That can seem like a kind of intellectual free-riding. Further, free-riding is often thought to be problematic. At the very least, we typically don't want to think of ourselves as free-riders. Having further motivated this objection, I'll argue that if intellectual outsourcing is a kind of free-riding, it isn't a problematic kind of free-riding. There is no free-riding problem here.

MOTIVATING THE OBJECTION

The faculty at my school have a union. The union works to protect the rights of the faculty, create equitable workplace conditions, and secure fair salaries, among other things. While the members of the union enjoy some benefits that are exclusive to union members, the union works for the causes on behalf of *all* faculty, whether they are members of the union or not. So, for instance, when the union bargains a salary increase, all faculty benefit from the union's efforts,

DOI: 10.4324/9781003369004-6

not just the union members. Of course, membership comes at a cost. People have to supply the funds that enable the union to do its work. When I joined the union, one of the motivating factors was that I didn't want to be a free-rider. While I would benefit from the union's efforts regardless of whether I contributed dues, it didn't feel right to reap this benefit at the expense of others without paying my fare share. For the union to succeed, it needed members to pay dues, and no faculty member had any greater responsibility to join and pay dues than any other. Given all of this, benefitting from the union while not paying my fair share didn't sit well with me. I didn't want to be a free-rider.

To take another example, suppose that there is a group of roommates. These roommates have decided not to divide up the chores in any explicit way, but all take responsibility to keep the common areas of the apartment in order. After all, they all have an interest in having a tidy apartment. In such a situation, however, we can easily imagine that a given roommate fails to pull his own weight. When there are dishes to be cleaned, he holds off knowing that someone else will get to it soon enough. When the trash is full, he stuffs a little more in without taking it out, since he knows someone else will take care of it eventually. This roommate isn't pulling his weight, but is freeloading off of his roommates. Such behavior is problematic and irresponsible. It exhibits a clearly objectionable kind of free-riding and shows how free-riding can be wrong.

Plausibly, we have a *prima facie* duty not to free-ride.[1] What that means is that in the absence of stronger reasons to do otherwise, we should not be free-riders. In discussing such a duty not to free-ride, Hrishikesh Joshi (2021) gives the example of a fisherman. This fisherman is part of a community that has a shared interest in not overfishing the local lake. However, if taking more fish than his fair share is the only way for this fisherman to feed his family, then his duty not to free-ride and exploit this common resource is overridden by his stronger duties to provide for his family. So, the duty not to free-ride can be overridden. That said, absent stronger reasons in the other direction, free-riding seems to be problematic.

How does this apply in the intellectual realm? For free-riding to occur here as well, we need two things: a common resource that benefits everyone, and an individual who fails to contribute their fair share to that resource (or who takes more than their fair share). In the intellectual realm, we can think of our shared resource as our shared pool of knowledge, or as Joshi (2021) has put it, "the epistemic commons." According to Joshi, the epistemic commons are a given community's collection of evidence, ideas, and knowledge. Thus, the epistemic commons are a shared *intellectual* resource. Since it is too much to ask of any one individual that they figure everything out for themselves, the epistemic commons allow each individual member to access the shared insights of the community. Intellectual communities consist of different members carrying out different intellectual projects – different people inquiring into different questions. This is particularly valuable since it would be impractical, if not impossible, for any one individual to do all of the relevant intellectual work for themselves. The epistemic commons allow for the entire community to benefit from the community's collective discoveries, from the answers that they have uncovered. We are all intellectually better off in virtue of having access to an epistemic commons. In addition, we are also often *practically* better off for this intellectual resource as well. Cars, vaccines, the internet, and electricity (to name just a few) all make our daily lives much better, and they are all the result of our epistemic commons. Our lives are made easier by the intellectual contributions of members of our community. As our understanding of the world has improved, so too has the quality of our lives. So, the epistemic commons offer benefits that extend beyond the intellectual realm as well. We thus also have a shared interest in having our epistemic commons well kept. We are all better off for sharing our intellectual endeavors, since the richer the intellectual collection is, the better off we all are. So, the epistemic commons are a valuable shared intellectual resource, one that helps keep a healthy intellectual environment in a community.

However, since the epistemic commons are a shared resource, there is at least the potential for free-riding. Individuals who benefit from the epistemic commons without also contributing their fair share might be thought to be intellectual free-riders. Such individuals are enjoying the benefits of a healthy epistemic commons without doing their part to maintain this shared resource. It might seem that such individuals are like the roommate who enjoys the tidy common areas of the apartment without actually doing any of the work to keep those areas neat and clean. Just as the roommate's free-riding behavior was seen to be problematic, it might look as though there is a problem with intellectual free-riding as well.[2]

Joshi's concern about maintaining the epistemic commons can also be related to our discussion of the wisdom of crowds in Chapter 1. Recall our discussion of the Condorcet Jury Theorem there. According to it, so long as individuals are reliable, adding their independent judgments together can provide strong reasons for the majority belief. For instance, polling the audience was a powerful lifeline on *Who Wants to be a Millionaire?* So, one way to make the case that everyone has a duty to contribute to the epistemic commons is by claiming that everyone should voice their own independent opinions. In so doing, they would help provide a valuable epistemic good for the community; they would be improving the reliability of the majority opinion.[3] Failing to do so could be seen as a kind of free-riding. Individuals who don't register their independent opinion would still gain the benefit of the group opinion without contributing their fair share. Further, the majority opinion would be less reliable in virtue of it consisting of fewer independent judgments. So, the community would also be worse off for such an individual's lack of involvement.

Now let's connect these concerns to our central conclusion. Our central conclusion claims that it is OK not to think for yourself, that novice individual inquiry is unnecessary. Some have seen this kind of epistemic dependence and intellectual outsourcing as a kind of free-riding, as a case where individuals are freely benefiting from the intellectual labors of others.[4] After all, individuals who think for themselves put in their own intellectual labor. They collect the relevant evidence, and they evaluate it. They come to conclusions and can then share those to the epistemic commons. In contrast, those who merely defer gain the intellectual fruits of those labors without themselves putting in any of the work. In the intellectual equivalent of 'give a penny, take a penny,' these individuals are only taking pennies.

Thomas Reid powerfully summarizes the worry as follows in his *Essays on the Powers of the Human Mind* (1827) as follows:

> As there are persons in the world of so mean and abject a spirit that they rather choose to owe their subsistence to the charity of others, than by industry to acquire some property of their own; so there are many more who may

be called mere beggars with regard to their opinions. Through laziness and indifference about the truth, they leave to others the drudgery of digging for this commodity; they can have enough at second hand to serve their occasions.

(339)

On this view, deferring is like intellectual begging. It is asking for an intellectual handout, and doing so in a situation where one simply doesn't want to put the work in themselves. It is free-riding on the intellectual labors of others, and it is defective. Obviously not all cases of begging are problematic. There are situations where this might be required or one's only real course of action. However, we do find begging problematic when the individual in question is fully capable of providing for themselves. Since our central conclusion is to apply to individuals who can think for themselves, yet choose not to, it might seem that the analogy here is apt. This, then, is the free-rider objection to our central conclusion.

THE COGNITIVE DIVISION OF LABOR

What can be said in response to the free-rider objection? The first thing to do is to note some important dissimilarities in the analogies previously mentioned. While intellectual outsourcing does bear some similarities to cases of problematic free-riding, there are several important differences to note. First of all, intellectual goods, unlike economic goods, can be freely distributed without creating any kind of scarcity.[5] When I get a cup of coffee from the office coffee pot, there is now less coffee for everyone else to have. When the fisherman leaves the lake with an excessive number of fish, things are made worse for others in the community who are relying on its fish. However, when I come to know something by relying on the epistemic commons, there is not thereby any less knowledge for everyone else to enjoy. My coming to know it on the basis of the intellectual efforts of others, does not take away, or diminish, their knowledge in any way, nor does it make it more difficult for anyone else to get this knowledge. No one individual is worse off for my gaining insights from the epistemic commons. Further, the community as a whole is not any worse off for my gaining from the epistemic commons. If anything, the community improves by way of having another member of it with an improved intellectual picture of the world. Educated communities are better off. They certainly are not worse off for having shared their knowledge with others in the community. So, there is an important difference between intellectual goods and economic goods. The fact that intellectual goods are not scarce goods makes the epistemic commons importantly different than other shared resources.

That said, the lack of scarcity may not take away all that is problematic about free-riding. Even if the shared goods don't diminish, there is still the fact that I am an unequal contributing member to the epistemic commons. I'm still not contributing my fair share, or pulling my intellectual weight, if I am relying extensively on others. So, even if my deference is not making others worse off by way of taking anything away from them, my lack of thinking for myself might still be problematic since I am not doing anything positive to contribute to the epistemic commons. Unequal participation in the epistemic commons may be thought to be problematic enough on its own, even if no one is worse off for it. It might just be unfair. For instance, one roommate's enjoyment of the clean commons area need not take away from any other roommate's enjoyment of those spaces. Enjoyment of a clean common area is not a scarce resource either. One roommate's enjoying the clean common area doesn't take away from anyone else's ability to enjoy it as well. So, the scarcity difference, while notable, does not look to be enough to eliminate everything that could be problematic about free-riding.

These considerations, however, do lead to another important difference between the epistemic commons and our problematic cases of free-riding. In our cases of problematic free-riding, each individual has something like an equal responsibility to contribute to the shared resource. When it came to the union, no faculty member had a greater obligation than any other to contribute dues. When it came to the clean apartment, no roommate had any greater responsibility than any other to keep the common areas in order. When there is an equal responsibility, failing to contribute amounts to problematic free-riding. If you are not contributing and you have an equal responsibility, you aren't doing your fair share and you are taking advantage of others. However, when it comes to the epistemic commons, we don't all share an equal responsibility for its maintenance and upkeep. Not only do we not all have an equal responsibility here, we shouldn't want everyone to be equal contributors to this shared resource.

The principal reason why there isn't an equal responsibility is that we have a cognitive division of labor. Let's first look at the division of labor more generally before zooming in on the cognitive division of labor. Groups succeed, and do better, by dividing up their tasks. Cultures have increased their productivity by distributing duties amongst their members. Rather than everyone growing their own food, making their own clothes, building their own homes, and so forth, we have groups that specialize in growing food, other groups that focus on making clothes, and yet other groups that build homes. It is easier to do one thing well then to do everything well. So, in dividing up labor, all the members of a community benefit. The same is true of our intellectual communities. We could all think about everything, but chances are we wouldn't think very well about all those things. So called 'Renaissance thinking' isn't a live option anymore given the vast array of things there are to think about. Intellectual specialization has taken over. We need biologists to think about biological matters, psychologists to think about human minds, chemists to think about matters of chemistry, and philosophers to think about philosophical questions. Just like those who focus on growing food become more likely to do it well, those who focus on thinking about biological matters become more likely to find the relevant answers. Specialization leads to expertise and expertise leads to more and better answers. While perhaps there was a time when someone could figure out pretty much anything that could be figured out for themselves, we no longer live in such a time. The 'Renaissance thinker' is no more.[6]

Let's look at an example. Hospitals are a common resource, but not everyone should be equally involved in the operation of a hospital. If you have to visit the emergency room, you don't want to have to worry who in the community happened to show up that day to do surgeries. While the hospital is a common resource, we all have an interest in having certain community members play an unequal role in its operation, particularly when it comes to medical procedures. Doctors and nurses should be disproportionately participating in the operation of a hospital. Equal participation in the hospital would make the hospital, and all of us, worse off, not better. If hospitals had equal participation, they would be less likely to serve their function. For similar reasons, we don't want our epistemic commons to be equally upkept by all. Just like not everyone is in the same position to contribute at the hospital, not everyone is in the same position to contribute to the epistemic commons. So, regarding the epistemic commons, equal participation would leave the commons in worse shape, not better.

The epistemic commons need to be maintained by the relevant experts. The community does best with regard to its biological knowledge, when it is the biologists who maintain that aspect of the epistemic commons. We do best with regard to our psychological knowledge when it is psychologists who are the chief contributors of psychological information. We are all familiar with the prescription "don't read the comments." Adding everyone's two-cents into the mix does not improve the intellectual offerings of the epistemic commons. The epistemic commons are better off with unequal involvement, where the relevant experts are the primary contributors regarding matters of their expertise.

Let's look at some other examples to further this point. I like to listen to music. I make use of a number of common musical resources: YouTube, Amazon Music, Spotify, etc. At the same time, I have not contributed any content to any of them. I don't make music, at least certainly not any worth listening to. I haven't made music since middle school band, and I'm not sure that even counts. Am I a musical free-rider given my unequal contribution to the musical commons? I don't think so, or at least, if I am, it isn't a problematic kind of free-riding. This is a perfectly fine way for me to live my musical life – enjoying the music of others while not contributing any music of my own. We shouldn't want everyone to be equal contributors to the musical commons. So, the fact that I benefit from the musical commons without contributing to it is not problematic.

I also like to eat good food. I enjoy going to restaurants and trying out new recipes at home. I greatly benefit from a number of culinary resources – the culinary commons, so to speak. While I do some cooking, I haven't made and distributed any of my own recipes. When it comes to recipes, I'm entirely a taker, not a giver. I am certainly not an equal contributor to the culinary commons. Does this make me a culinary free-rider? I don't think so, or again, if I am, I don't think that this is a problematic kind of free-riding. Here too, unequal contributions are perfectly fine.

So, how does all of this apply to intellectual outsourcing and the epistemic commons? What makes the intellectual case more like the music and food cases, rather than like the union and roommate cases, is that in the intellectual case there is not an equally shared responsibility to the common resource. Whereas each roommate has an equal responsibility to keep the apartment clean, we don't all have an equal responsibility to make music, make food, or make intellectual discoveries. If those are things that someone wants to do, then that's great. You are, and should be, free to do any of those things. However, if that's not your thing, it's OK not to do so as well. There is nothing wrong with failing to do any of these things. Further, not contributing to the common collection of music, food, or knowledge does not preclude you from unproblematically enjoying the contributions of others in these areas.

There are plenty of different ways to live your life in society, and living your life well in society does not require you to contribute to each and every aspect of society. Perhaps there would be something wrong if you didn't contribute to *any* aspect of society while you were perfectly able to do so. But, that is not our concern here. Of concern here is simply whether you can be a contributing healthy member of society without contributing to the epistemic commons – this shared intellectual resource. Surely you can be. We don't need to all do a little bit of everything. It is fine to specialize, and if you choose to contribute to society in ways that aren't intellectual that is a perfectly fine way to be a member of society. A healthy society needs individuals like that too.

In addition, the epistemic commons are not improved by simply anyone's contributions. This goes back to the idea that we don't all have an equal and shared responsibility here. Novice inquiry will not improve the state of the epistemic commons. To further see the importance of specialization and unequal contribution to the epistemic commons, it will be helpful to explore the notion of epistemic trespassing.

EPISTEMIC TRESPASSING

Epistemic trespassing occurs when someone passes judgment on matters outside of their area of expertise.[7] While both experts and novices can trespass, the literature on epistemic trespassing has focused on experts who transgress the boundaries of their expertise, yet nevertheless proceed to make proclamations. Ballantyne (2019: 195) gives the example of Linus Pauling as a paradigm case of an epistemic trespasser. Pauling was a well-renowned chemist who even won a Nobel Prize for his groundbreaking work in chemistry. While an expert chemist, Pauline went on to also advocate for megadoses of vitamin C as a treatment for cancer. Not only were such claims false, and vehemently rejected by the relevant experts, what made them an instance of trespassing is that they were claims firmly outside of Pauling's area of expertise. Pauling had no relevant training here.

While what is relevant to our issue is novice, rather than expert, trespassing, examining what is wrong with expert trespassing will nonetheless illuminate what is problematic with novice trespassing as well. Two notable consequences of expert trespassing are that i) trespassers lead novices astray, and ii) they create messes that the true experts must then clean up.[8]

Let's look at each consequence in turn. This first consequence has to do with the cognitive division of labor again. Novices rely on experts to know things within their domain of expertise, and to be able to communicate those things to the rest of us. Responsible experts must be cognizant of this, and responsive to this epistemic dependence of others. As DiPaolo (2022) makes this point,

> [e]xpert testimony is both an assertion and a sort of command. The epistemic authority behind genuine expert testimony is analogous to the authority behind a command. Just as someone issuing a command confers a responsibility on the person receiving it, when someone delivers expert testimony to a novice, they confer a responsibility on the novice to believe what's asserted.
>
> (237)

So, in making their proclamations, experts invite novices to trust them at their word. When this proclamation is made outside of their area of expertise, the expert misleads those who are relying on them for their expertise. Epistemic trespassing is thus a crime of negligence.[9] Trespassers take advantage of those who are relying on experts, whether they do so knowingly or not. Novices rely on expert opinion, and when the epistemic commons are littered with non-expert opinions that are not easily discernable from legitimate expert opinions, these intellectual dependents are harmed.

Another example of an epistemic trespasser is Scott Atlas. DiPaolo (2022) notes that Atlas was a radiologist with no epidemiological expertise, yet used his role as advisor to the Trump administration's Coronavirus Task Force to denounce mask-wearing in favor of spreading COVID-19 to reach herd immunity. (224) So, like Pauling, Atlas wandered outside of his area of expertise. In both cases the proclamations of the trespassers resulted in individuals getting false beliefs. Those who believed Pauling and Atlas ended up with mistaken beliefs. But things are worse than that. The consequences in both of these cases were not merely intellectual. These trespassers also affected how people lived their lives and their personal well-being.

In addition, in littering the epistemic commons, trespassers also divert the attention of the relevant experts away from more important work. When experts trespass, those who actually have expertise in the given domain must then take the time to clean up the epistemic commons from the mess left by trespassers. Trespassers can create misinformation, cause unnecessary confusion, and damage relations of trust with the public. Genuine experts are left to clean up this mess, correcting misinformation, clearing up confusion, and building back trust in the community. Since we are all finite creatures, any efforts spent on these tasks take away from intellectual work that could be done elsewhere. It would be better if the experts could focus on answering new questions and expanding our knowledge in their domain of expertise rather than doing damage control. Returning to the case of Pauling, a great deal of medical experts' time, energy, and resources were spent refuting Pauling's claims about vitamin C. These valuable expert resources would have been better utilized if they were not needed to clean up the epistemic commons.

These problematic consequences occur when experts trespass and go to show what is wrong with expert trespassing. Expert trespassing is plausibly more problematic than novice trespassing. The expert trespasser still trespasses with a kind of expertise, and their legitimate expertise can make it easier to mask their lack of expertise in the domain in which they are trespassing. For instance, when a physicist trespasses into the domain of philosophy, their trespassing will likely be less apparent than when an all-around novice does so. When Novice Norman weighs in on his views about free will, other lay people are much less likely to mistake his views as expert opinion as when a highly regarded physicist does so.

While novice trespassers are less likely to be mistaken for experts, this is not to say that their trespassing has no negative effects. Novice proclamations can still muddy the intellectual waters and create unnecessary confusion in the epistemic commons. Minimally, we are not intellectually better off when everyone is chiming in about everything.[10] The recent COVID-19 pandemic makes this point clear. Not only did we suffer from experts in one field trespassing outside of their domain of expertise and thereby creating unnecessary confusion, but those with no nearby expertise were also highly responsible for the spread of misinformation and the resulting confusion. After all, people's views are not only shaped by those who they view as experts. One way that such novice influence can occur is through familiarity bias. Familiarity bias refers to the fact that a claim merely seeming familiar to us makes it seem more plausible to us. Thus, when we frequently confront a claim, the mere fact that it becomes familiar to us will also make it seem more plausible. The more plausible it seems, the more likely we are to believe it. Familiarity bias has ramifications, whether or not the source is seen as an expert.

Continued exposure to a given novice claim can make that very claim seem more plausible, even without anyone confusing the non-experts for experts. So, novice trespassers too can also damage the epistemic commons.

THE WISDOM OF CROWDS AGAIN

Before wrapping up, we need to return to think about the wisdom of crowds. Recall that individual opinions can make the group more reliable, even when those individuals lack expertise. So, don't individuals who fail to think for themselves thereby make the majority opinion less reliable and thus harm the intellectual community? And if so, don't they thereby have a duty to do so? Everything we have said so far in response to the free-riding objection still fails to address the problem when it is coupled with the wisdom of crowds. So, what can be said in response here?

First, an individual's independent opinion will only be epistemically valuable if they are reliable on the matter at hand – if they are more likely than not to have a true belief. One worry here concerns how often this is the case for novices. Consider the following: Are you more likely than not to have a true (and independent) belief about climate change? About the nature of free will? About the chemical composition of caffeine? If you are like me, then I have my doubts. Many issues have extensive bodies of evidence that we are unaware of. In addition, these bodies of evidence often need significant skill to interpret and evaluate. So, the odds of getting it right on your own are often not very good. Further, when considering whether your judgment on the matter would be reliable, you can wonder about how reliable you are in determining that as well! That is, are you reliable at determining whether you are reliable about the matter at hand? It can be difficult to even tell whether one's independent opinion would be valuable, and there are good empirical reasons to doubt our abilities here as well. We don't know what we don't know, and this can create problems. Dunning (2022) outlines several ways that individuals have a hard time grasping what they don't know. Dunning cites empirical evidence that we overclaim knowledge (claim to know about things that don't in fact exist), have illusions of understanding (think we understand things until we are asked to explain them), and fall prey to the Dunning–Kruger effect. The Dunning–Kruger effect is the idea that the less that one knows in a domain, the more likely they are to believe that they are knowledgeable in that domain.[11] So, when we lack the knowledge and competence in a domain, we are bad at determining whether we are knowledgeable and competent in that domain. In brief, we are often blissfully unaware of our own incompetence; our ignorance is often invisible to us.[12] So, there are good reasons to doubt our ability to judge our reliability in matters where we lack expertise, and we should be cautious in thinking that our own novice opinions are reliable. While the Condorcet Jury Theorem shows that aggregating opinions *can* make the majority belief rational, we need to be cautious in our applications of it in the real world.[13] In particular, we shouldn't exaggerate its applicability. After all, the theorem concerns quite idealized conditions, conditions that are difficult to determine whether (and to what extent) they apply in real-world cases. Finally, even in cases where it is clear that one's independent opinion would be of benefit to the epistemic commons, it is another matter to say that they are thereby *required* to contribute it. Even if it would be epistemically better if they did, it is doubtful that we are required to always do what is epistemically the best. So, even in cases where things would be epistemically better if one thought for themselves, it does not follow that they are required to do so.[14] For these reasons, the insights concerning the wisdom of crowds are insufficient to save the free-riding objection to our central conclusion.

In this chapter we have explored the free-rider objection. We have seen reasons to think that in not thinking for yourself, you free-ride off of the epistemic commons – that you fail to contribute your fair share. What we have seen, however, is that there isn't an equal responsibility to contribute to the epistemic commons, and where there isn't an equal responsibility, free-riding either doesn't occur or it isn't problematic. The reason we don't have an equal responsibility to maintain the epistemic commons has to do with the cognitive division of labor. The epistemic commons, and the community that relies on it, are each better off when the commons are maintained by the relevant experts, not by equal contributions by everyone.

What we have seen is that the requirement for individuals to contribute to the epistemic commons in areas outside of their expertise is a requirement for them to commit epistemic trespassing. Making proclamations outside of one's area of expertise is epistemic trespassing, and we've seen why it is problematic. The objection on offer, therefore, implies that those who do not commit epistemic trespassing are intellectual free-riders of a problematic sort. This is implausible. Having examined the intellectual division of labor and the problems that occur from epistemic trespassing, we can see that such a conclusion is simply false. While the wrongs that occur from novice trespassing may be less severe than when experts trespass, these considerations are sufficient to show what is wrong with the free-rider objection. After all, we do not need to establish the conclusion that it is *wrong* for novices to contribute to the epistemic commons, simply that it isn't *necessary* – that it's OK if they don't. So, the free-rider objection fails.

With the free-rider objection answered, in the next chapter we will examine yet another objection to our central conclusion – the Socratic objection. According to it, our central conclusion has a more limited application than we have been letting on. While there are many domains where it is perfectly fine to defer to others, some domains are such that it is essential to think about things for yourself. For instance, while there may be nothing wrong with deferring to a chemist about the chemical composition of caffeine, many see something problematic about deferring about matters of morality, aesthetics, politics, and philosophy.

In the last chapter we saw that not everyone has an equal responsibility to maintain the epistemic commons. The epistemic commons go best when they are maintained by the relevant experts — by those who are best positioned to know the answers. That said, it might be thought that some questions are such that *everyone* should wrestle with them. Perhaps some questions simply shouldn't be outsourced. As Socrates famously claimed, "the unexamined life is not worth living." According to the objection to be considered in this chapter, while there is nothing problematic about deference in most domains, questions in certain domains deserve everyone's attention. Regarding some questions, we simply must think for ourselves. The idea here is that while I can, and should, outsource my medical diagnosis to my doctor, I should not outsource inquiry into questions like 'how should I live my life?' Questions of morality, aesthetics, religion, politics, and philosophy more generally have all been thought to be such that individuals need to wrestle with them for themselves. In what follows, we will call questions in these domains 'Socratic questions' and call these domains of inquiry 'Socratic domains' for ease of expression.

In this chapter, we will examine a number of different rationales that have been given for treating questions in

DOI: 10.4324/9781003369004-7

Socratic domains as special – as questions that are not to be outsourced. What all these versions of the Socratic objection have in common is that they claim that the morals drawn from the argument from expertise and the argument from evidential swamping don't apply to a particular set of questions – Socratic questions. Where they differ is in the reasons why Socratic questions are to be treated differently. Having motivated each version of the objection, we will see that each fails. What we will see is that there is no good reason to treat Socratic questions as immune from our central conclusion. It is OK not to think about Socratic questions for yourself.

Before looking at the individual versions of the Socratic objection separately, let's first examine some shared motivation for this concern.

MOTIVATING THE OBJECTION

Finding out the best route to a new location is easy to do. You simply plug the address into an app like Google Maps and you get your answer. There is no need to spend time investigating the map for yourself, and there is nothing deficient about someone who relies solely on the app for their navigation needs. Outsourcing the project to Google Maps is a great way to find the answer, and one that is routinely relied upon. What if, however, Google developed a different app, Google Morals, to help you navigate the moral terrain?[1] When confronted with a moral problem, you simply plug the issue into Google Morals, and it tells you what you should do. Whenever you are in a morally tricky situation, or are confronting a novel moral issue, just ask the app what to do. While most find relying on Google Maps entirely unproblematic, many philosophers have been uneasy with the idea of similarly relying on something

Why It's OK Not to Think for Yourself

like Google Morals. Outsourcing questions of morality seems to many to be importantly different than outsourcing questions of driving directions. That is, something seems odd or inappropriate about such deference.

The uneasiness that one might feel with using Google Morals carries over to questions outside the moral domain as well. What is the meaning of life? Does God exist? Is this artwork beautiful? Questions like these have been at the heart of human existence. They concern what it means to be human and what consequences that has for our lives. Questions like these, it may be thought, are ones that are essential to think about for yourself – questions that cannot be left unexamined.

A number of philosophers have argued that there is something problematic about accepting a moral belief merely on the basis of someone else's say-so.[2] Others have argued that something is amiss with accepting someone else's aesthetic testimony.[3] Still others have argued for a similar conclusion regarding political claims,[4] religious claims,[5] and philosophical claims more generally.[6] Here is a sample of the kinds of worries expressed.

In his book *In Defense of Anarchism* (1970), Robert Paul Wolff writes:

> The responsible man [sic] is not capricious or anarchic, for he does acknowledge himself [as] bound by moral constraints. But he insists that he alone is the judge of those constraints. He may listen to the advice of others, but he makes it his own by determining for himself whether it is good advice ... He may do what another tells him, but not because he has been told to do it.
>
> (13)

Similarly, Kant in his *Critique of Judgement* (2005) declares:

> If a man ... does not find a building, a prospect, or a poem beautiful, a hundred voices all highly praising it will not force his innermost agreement ... he clearly sees that the agreement of others gives no valid proof of the judgment about beauty ... that a thing has pleased others could never serve as the basis for an aesthetical judgment.
>
> (94)

Regarding morality, Allison Hills (2009) claims the following: "Once you have reached maturity as an adult and have the ability to think about moral questions by yourself [...] you have strong reasons to do so, indeed that refusing to do so is unacceptable." (95)

In addition, Cassam (2018) highlights the distinctiveness of these Socratic domains, suggesting that whereas we must defer to scientists, everyone should assess the claims of those working in the humanities for themselves.[7]

So, many find there to be something distinctive about Socratic questions, something that makes deference in these Socratic domains problematic. At the very least, accepting such testimony seems to raise issues that are not raised by other, more ordinary, cases of deference. Is there something wrong with deference in Socratic domains, or do our initial impressions deceive us? In what follows we will critically examine several different explanations that have been offered for why we should treat Socratic questions differently. While we will touch on Socratic questions as a whole, our focus will be with moral deference in particular, since that has also been the focus of much of the relevant literature. In addition, moral deference provides perhaps the strongest case against our central conclusion.

NORMATIVE QUESTIONS

A number of authors distinguish between cases of testimony concerning purely moral matters and testimony concerning mixed moral matters.[8] This distinction is due to McGrath. As she makes the distinction, cases of pure moral deference occur when deference is made on the basis of "purely moral information that one lacks." (2009: 322) So, in cases of pure moral deference, the deferring party is aware of all the relevant empirical information. Their deference is solely about the moral features of the situation. In contrast, cases of impure moral deference occur when the hearer lacks both moral and non-moral (the relevant empirical) information. The problem with moral deference is thought to occur, or at least be strongest, regarding cases of pure moral deference. That the problem is felt most strongly concerning pure moral deference lends credibility to the idea that there is something problematic about deferring on normative matters. Normative matters are evaluative matters, they concern assessments of value like that something is good/bad, better/worse, valuable or not. According to our first version of the Socratic objection, what is problematic about moral deference is that it is a kind of normative deference.

In addition to morality, aesthetic matters are also normative matters. Aesthetic judgments and moral judgments both involve applying evaluative standards. So, an appeal to normativity could explain what is wrong with both moral and aesthetic deference – two of our Socratic domains. However, not all Socratic questions are normative questions. For instance, questions concerning God's existence or whether humans have free will are not normative questions.[9] Nevertheless, deference on these matters often comes with the same kind of uneasiness that some people feel regarding moral deference. So, the idea that there is something problematic about normative deference fails to capture at least all of the intended verdicts. In addition, however, there are cases of normative deference that seem perfectly fine. It seems perfectly appropriate for me to defer to Emily Post on matters of etiquette, yet matters of etiquette are also normative matters. They too concern applying an evaluative standard, yet such deference does not seem to be problematic in any way. In addition, it appears to be perfectly appropriate to defer on many other normative matters. For instance, it is fine to defer to a logician about what follows from what, to defer to a lawyer about what legal strategy one should pursue, to defer to my wife about whether this tie goes with this shirt, to defer to a financial planner on how one should invest, and so forth. All of these issues are normative issues, they each concern what you should and should not do, yet none of them carry with them the feeling of uneasiness that many feel regarding moral deference. So, the explanation that what is amiss with deferring on Socratic questions is that they are normative, is not a very good explanation of our phenomenon. A question being normative is neither necessary nor sufficient for the alleged problem with deference to occur.[10]

One last thing to note here is that it is quite implausible that we are ever in situations of pure moral deference.[11] After all, how often do non-experts share all of the relevant empirical information with the experts? Take for instance the issue of eating meat from factory farms.[12] While a novice might have some awareness of what factory farms are like, or their prevalence, or something about the physiological effects on animals and the ramifications on the environment, the relevant experts are likely to be far more informed about the relevant empirical details. Those who have extensively studied the issue will have a vast amount of empirical information that is unlikely to be shared by a mere novice inquirer. Such an inequality in empirical information, however, makes such cases of deference impure cases. So, even if there was a problem with pure moral deference, it wouldn't be a problem that we often confront.

NO RELEVANT EXPERTS

According to this second version of the Socratic objection, Socratic questions are distinctive because unlike questions in other domains, there are no experts in matters of morality, aesthetics, religion, politics, and philosophy. Why might expertise in Socratic domains not exist? In what follows, we will look at three possible accounts as to why there would not be any experts in Socratic domains. Our first account claims that answers to these questions are equally accessible to everyone. Experts are those who are more likely to be able to find answers to questions in their area of expertise. So, if the answers to Socratic questions are equally accessible to all, expertise in these domains simply would not exist. If all of us are on a level playing field in terms of answering Socratic questions, then there are no experts in Socratic domains.

Why think that these matters are equally accessible to everyone? One proposal is that these matters are *a priori*. Questions that are *a priori* are questions that can be answered apart from any experience. You can find answers to *a priori* questions just by thinking about them. Does 2+2=4? To figure that out, you just need to think about it. No investigation out there in the world is necessary. Similarly, once you have a full description of a case, all that remains to determine whether a given action is morally right or wrong is simply to think about it.[13] The moral truths are just out there for anyone to discover by thinking about them. No empirical investigation is necessary. If Socratic questions have *a priori* answers, then it might be thought that these answers are equally available to all – it just takes a little thinking.

However, as McGrath (2009: 324–5) has argued, even if *a priori* truths are equally 'out there' for everyone to find (i.e. no one is precluded from discovering them), it does not follow that everyone is in an equally good epistemic position to find these truths. Training, intelligence, and skills are all relevant to finding *a priori* truths, and we are not all equal with regard to these intellectual factors. There are people who are much more informed about moral issues, are more familiar with the relevant considerations, have spent more time thinking about them, are more careful thinkers, and so forth. These features make them more likely to find the moral truths, even if the moral truths are equally 'out there' to be found by anyone. For instance, mathematics is also an *a priori* discipline. The answers to mathematical questions are equally 'out there' for anyone to discover – they too just take some thinking. Discovering mathematical answers does not depend upon having had certain experiences; they can be discovered just by thinking about them. However, it is clear that we are not all in an equally good epistemic position to find mathematical answers. In particular, mathematicians are far more likely to find answers to questions in their domain than novices are. While the answers are *a priori*, the training, intelligence, skills, and so forth of mathematicians help them find those answers much more easily than the rest of us.[14] If you are still unsure about this, take your best crack at proving a complicated mathematical theorem on your own. If you are like me, you'll find the fact that the answer is *a priori* of little comfort in finding it.

These considerations call for a shift in the objection. Perhaps what is relevant is not that moral answers *a priori*, but that they are also self-evident. Self-evident truths are simply obvious, like that every golden trumpet is a trumpet. So, according to this line of thought, moral truths are intellectually low hanging fruit, right there for the taking for anyone who is interested. This feature would distinguish moral claims from the more complex mathematical claims. While mathematical claims are *a priori*, only the very simple ones are self-evident (e.g. $1+1=2$). What might account for the difference? Well, perhaps moral claims are imprinted on us all in our conscience. Complex mathematical claims are not so imprinted. This could explain why moral claims are self-evident while complex mathematical claims are not. Thomas Reid (1785/1983) puts forward this kind of view when he claims the following:

> the whole system of moral conduct follows so easily, and with so little aid of reasoning, that every man of common understanding, who wishes to know his duty, may know it. The path of duty is a plain path, which the upright in heart can rarely mistake. Such it must be, since every man is bound to walk in it. There are some intricate cases in morals which admit of disputation; but these seldom occur in practice; and when they do, the learned disputant has no great advantage
>
> ... In order to know what is right and what is wrong in human conduct, we need only listen to the dictates of our conscience, when the mind is calm and unruffled, or attend to the judgment we form of others in like circumstances.

(359–60)

More recently, Smith has claimed that such a view of moral claims is intimately connected to the very ability to live a moral life. As he puts it, "our moral life seems to presuppose that [moral] facts are in principle available to all; that no one in particular is better placed to discover them than anyone else." (1994: 5)

On this view, it is not merely the fact that moral claims are *a priori* that makes moral deference problematic. Rather, it is the fact that the moral truths are so easily apprehended that explains what is problematic about moral deference. If you could just as easily access the moral truth yourself, then deference would at least seem bizarre, if not lazy. That said, this explanation presents an implausible view of the relation between human minds and moral truths. If moral truths were so obvious, we simply wouldn't confront the vast amount of moral disagreement that we do. Moral disagreement is extensive, widespread, and persistent. If moral truths were low hanging fruit that is so easily grasped, this simply wouldn't be the case. For instance, unlike many moral claims, the claim that every golden trumpet is a trumpet just doesn't inspire much controversy. So much for the idea that there are no moral experts since morality is equally accessible to us all. Moral claims being *a priori* doesn't help with the problem, and their being self-evident just isn't plausible.

A second way in which there may be no relevant experts is if Socratic questions have subjective answers – if there is no objective fact of the matter to answers in these domains. For instance, it is often claimed that beauty is in the eye of the beholder. If beauty is in the eye of the beholder, then deference about matters of beauty would be problematic. On such a picture of beauty, it is only one's own standards of beauty that matter, and no one's standards are any better or more correct than anyone else's. On such a picture, deferring on a matter of beauty would make little sense.[15] If anything, doing so would make one *less* likely to get at the truth since it would be moving away from the only standards that matter (one's own). Similarly, if morality is more like a matter of taste, and is something that is relative to individuals, we could account for why moral deference is problematic. Each individual person would be best positioned to determine the truth of any moral claim for themselves, since the truth of that moral claim would be relative to that individual. While such an ethical subjectivism would explain why moral deference is unlike other kinds of deference, ethical subjectivism is not a very plausible view of morality.[16] In brief, such a picture of morality has it that we cannot legitimately criticize the actions of others and that each of us is morally infallible. Both consequences are implausible. In addition to the implausibility of ethical subjectivism, such an explanation fails to carry over to the other Socratic domains in question. Questions about whether God exists, whether humans have free will, and what it takes for a belief to be rational are all clearly objective matters. If God exists, then God exists for everyone, whether they believe it or not. Similarly, if God does not exist, then God does not exist for anyone, regardless of their attitudes on the matter. So, while the subjectivist explanation might have some plausibility in the domain of aesthetics, it fails to account for what would be problematic about moral, religious, and philosophical deference more generally.[17]

A third, and final, threat to expertise in Socratic domains comes from the extensive disagreement in them. As was mentioned earlier, matters of morality are highly contentious. Ethicists disagree about a wide range of cases and theories. Religious disagreement, political disagreement, and philosophical disagreement more generally are also commonplace. Further, the disagreements only seem to be increasing, rather than decreasing, as new views emerge providing new opportunities for disagreement. Doesn't such extensive disagreement threaten expertise? If there were genuine experts in these domains, we might expect for there to be a convergence of opinion – for the experts to have collaboratively figured a bunch of things out by now. However, in Socratic domains, that doesn't seem to be the case. In Socratic domains we are often still wrestling with the same questions we were thousands of years ago. So, perhaps what explains what seems wrong with deference in these domains is that there are no real experts to defer to, as evidenced by the widespread disagreement.

To respond to this version of the objection, we need to remember how we are thinking of expertise. Experts are those who are in a significantly better epistemic position on the topic at hand. Given all the disagreement in these domains, we know that there are a lot of false beliefs in these domains. However, experts can have false beliefs, they are not infallible. What matters is whether they are still significantly more likely than the rest of us to have a true belief. Given that putative experts in these domains have amassed a vast amount of background knowledge, honed their skills at evaluating arguments and objections in these fields, and have spent a great deal of time thinking about these issues, they *are* much more likely than the rest of us to get at the answers. Now it might be that the expert philosopher still isn't very likely to get to the philosophical truth. While the track-record of any given philosopher might not be all that impressive, our conception of expertise is essentially contrastive.[18] Given their background, they are still much more likely than we are to discover the answers.[19]

Let's look at a practical analogy. Expert baseball players are at best only 33% likely to get a hit on any occasion (at least when being pitched to by a professional). However, while their track-record here is significantly under 0.500, they are still far more likely to get a hit in such a situation than a non-expert. So, even with such a somewhat diminished track-record, in the interest of getting a hit, going with the expert baseball player is the way to go. Similarly, even if the track-record of experts in Socratic domains is not all that impressive, they are still significantly better positioned to determine the answers to questions in those domains than non-experts are.

The imagined objector might make a small shift here. They may grant that unreliable experts are still experts but insist that they should not be deferred to, given their suspect track-records. After all, why should we defer to an unreliable inquirer? We shouldn't, but this doesn't tell against our central conclusion. The unreliability of experts does not give a novice a stronger reason to think for themselves on the matter at hand. After all, novices are in an even *worse* epistemic position to determine the answer to the question at hand than the unreliable expert! So, novice inquiry into such questions will be even *more* unreliable. That's hardly the way to go. If anything, the unreliability of the experts in a domain gives us reason to suspend judgment on the issues in that domain, but it won't give us a reason to think for ourselves.

In some ways, this is simply an extension of the argument from evidential swamping. Recall that according to the argument from evidential swamping, when a matter is suitably contentious amongst the relevant experts, the rational thing for us to do is to suspend judgment. So, given that conclusion, there would be something amiss with believing what any one expert in these domains believed about a contentious matter. When a debate is in a state of disarray amongst the relevant experts, it is not rational to defer to any one of them. The rational thing to do is to suspend judgment. If those who are best positioned (epistemically speaking) to answer some question cannot do so with any type of consensus, then a rational answer is simply unavailable to the novice. So, we can agree with the explanation here, that on contentious issues in these domains we should not simply defer to any one expert. When the debate amongst the experts is in a state of disarray, the thing to do is to suspend judgment, and thinking for yourself won't change that.

It also should be noted that while Socratic domains are rife with disagreements, we shouldn't exaggerate things. There are still many matters in these domains that enjoy widespread agreement. For instance, while many moral claims are highly contentious, some moral claims enjoy widespread consensus (e.g. torturing innocent children to pass the time is wrong). While different ethicists might give different explanations for why such a terrible action is wrong, there is widespread agreement that it is.[20] So, we shouldn't be too quick to exaggerate the disagreements in these domains. We focus on contentious moral issues since there is more to discuss there, but there is also plenty of moral agreement lying in the background. Further, widespread controversy is not unique to Socratic domains. Some empirical matters enjoy the same kind of contentiousness as morality, politics, and religion. For example, think about the current state of quantum mechanics to give just one example. So, even if this diagnosis did succeed, it would fail to divide the cases in the intended way; it wouldn't neatly divide the Socratic domains from the rest. So, this explanation also fails to give us a reason to treat Socratic domains differently, it fails to show why we must think for ourselves about Socratic questions.

So much for versions of the objection that claim that there are no experts in Socratic domains. We have seen good reason to resist each of these accounts. However, we have not yet exhausted the ways of motivating the Socratic objection.

THE IMPORTANCE OF GETTING IT RIGHT

Some questions might be so important that they simply aren't the kinds of things that a responsible person would outsource to someone else. Recall Socrates' declaration that "the unexamined life is not worth living." Plausibly, to examine your life is to inquire about certain questions, and to do so on your own, not simply taking someone else's word for it. Here the thought is that there are questions that are so important, or central to human flourishing or well-being, that everyone should be thinking for themselves about these questions. Anyone who fails to think for themselves about these questions would be conducting their intellectual lives in a problematic way. When there is so much on the line (i.e. whether God exists, how you should live your life, etc.), there is simply no room for deference. At least, not according to the objection here.[21]

However, the importance of getting it right actually points in the other direction. What the argument from expertise showed us is that we are more likely to get the answer right by deferring to the relevant experts. When matters are particularly important, the strategy for getting to the truth doesn't change. If anything, it is reinforced. When the stakes are at their highest, we have all the more reason to take the best available route to the answer, and as we saw, that is deference to the relevant experts. So, the importance of the issue at hand does not show that we should think for ourselves.

Further, this explanation fails to divide the cases in the intended way anyway. For instance, let's look at a purely empirical matter. Suppose you are faced with diffusing a bomb. Needless to say, it is very important that you get it right. Your life depends on it! As in the usual Hollywood setup, there are two wires: a red wire and a blue wire. Of course, you should cut the wire that diffuses the bomb, and not the one that causes it to immediately detonate. But which one is that? While it is a purely empirical matter (a matter of cause and effect), the importance of getting it right here does not make deference inappropriate. Unless you are a bomb expert yourself, thinking about the matter for yourself is ill-advised, especially when deference to an expert is an option. Deference to the relevant experts is definitely the way to go. The importance of getting it right here only strengthens the reasons to defer. If nothing really hung on the matter, then perhaps there would be more leeway. But here, lives are at stake. It would be irresponsible not to take the best route to the answer, and the best route to the answer is to outsource your inquiry.

MORAL VIRTUE

Another diagnosis of our phenomenon is that even if moral deference is perfectly fine, intellectually speaking, it is still *morally* deficient. Why might moral deference be morally deficient? Part of the explanation is that beliefs acquired by deference are isolated from the rest of one's character. From a virtue ethical perspective, virtuous actions are right actions performed for the right reasons and with the right accompanying motivations. So, even if deference can give you a true belief about what the right action is, you are still left without the right reasons and the right motivation. Virtue, it might be thought, requires a kind of 'subjective integration' and moral beliefs that are gained by deference preclude this.[22] If so, then moral deference leaves you unable to act virtuously and it does not help you to cultivate a virtuous character either. Given this, it might be thought that there are moral reasons not to defer about morality; doing so gets in the way of the cultivation of your moral virtue.[23]

To help fill out this worry, here are some issues that Howell (2014: 403) sees with moral deference:

- Deference indicates that the subject lacks certain virtues (given their need to defer).
- Deference bypasses the subject's own moral character.
- Moral beliefs gained by deference fail to integrate with the subject's other cognitive states which prevents them from achieving higher degrees of virtue.
- Deference can either undermine the development of moral virtues since the subject is unlikely to be able to reliably act in accordance with the virtue.

Howell sees the most telling difference between appealing to Google Maps and appealing to Google Morals as regarding what such deference indicates about the subject. Needing to defer on the directions to a new location does not indicate any troubling informational deficit on the part of the subject, whereas needing to defer about the wrongness of an action does. For instance, we would find it troubling if we found out that someone needed to defer to an authority about whether torture is wrong. We expect them to have been able to figure that out for themselves. So, on this account, moral deference is problematic because it indicates a problematic state of the subject. The subject, in needing to defer, shows their moral defect or deficit on their part.

Howell's proposal gives two separable diagnoses of what is wrong with moral deference: i) it indicates a morally non-ideal state of the subject, and ii) deferring cannot give the subject all that they need (or all that they should want). Regarding the first, the need for deference indicates a lack of moral virtue. Regarding the second, moral deference can only give the subject a true belief (or knowledge), not moral virtue. Deference will *not* give the subject the requisite reasons or emotions that are required for exercising the relevant moral virtue. So, deference does not equip our subject to become virtuous.

This second explanation may also be able to accommodate what is wrong with deference in other Socratic domains like aesthetics and religion. If aesthetic judgments, or religious judgments, also have key emotional components to them, then those components will not transfer to the hearer through deference.[24] In gaining a true belief (or even knowledge), our subject will still be missing those key components to the relevant aesthetic or religious states. So, aesthetic deference, and religious deference, could also fail to deliver all that is needed by the subject if in these domains, more is required than simply getting it right − if it is more than simply an intellectual matter.[25]

What can be said about this explanation about what is problematic about Socratic deference? We need to be careful in thinking about what this proposal both does and does not show. First, it *does* show why we might be uncomfortable with Socratic deference, and moral deference in particular. Such deference indicates a deficit on the part of the subject. So, the need to defer indicates that the subject is in some sub-optimal state. Things are not as they should be. So, moral deference indicates a sub-optimal state in the deferring individual. However, this fact alone *does not* show that moral deference (and other types of Socratic deference) should not be done. If our subject needs to defer on a matter of morality, then that indicates that they lack the relevant moral virtues. That's not ideal, but what should such an agent do? Given that they have a moral question that they are trying to answer, and they lack the relevant moral virtues to determine the answer, it seems like deference is precisely what they should be doing! While they are in a sub-optimal moral state, deference is still the way to go. Perhaps especially because they are in a morally deficient state, deference is the way to go. Pointing out what is lacking in a subject who needs to defer does nothing to indict their deference. We may want things to be different, but given that they aren't, deference is perfectly appropriate. So, the fact that deference shows a deficit in the hearer does not show that deference should not be done. This point carries over to cases of deference more generally. If a subject is going to defer, then they lack the answer to their question. So, they are in a sub-optimal informational state. It would be better if they already knew the answer. But, given that they do not already know the answer, what should they do? Here too they should take a good route to that answer, and deference is such a route.

Similarly, while moral deference may not give the subject all that they want, or need, it still puts them on the right path. It is true that you cannot simply become virtuous by deference. Moral virtue requires more than a true belief about the moral status of the action in question. However, if you don't even have that, then deference is still the way to go. Even if it would be better if you were virtuous, given that you aren't, you might as well get a true belief about what you should do. Deference at least provides one of the essential elements of moral virtue – the correct judgment. While more is still needed, this too doesn't tell against improving one's current situation. So, the explanation from moral virtue also fails to show what is wrong with moral deference.

IN FAVOR OF SOCRATIC DEFERENCE

While we have seen reasons to reject each of the proposals for explaining what is wrong with Socratic deference, and moral deference in particular, the reader may not yet be convinced that such deference is unproblematic. So, let's briefly set out the case for Socratic deference. The foundation for the case has already been made in the argument from expertise and the argument from evidential swamping. We should treat similar cases alike, and given that there are truths in these domains, and that not everyone is in an equally good epistemic position to determine these truths, deference looks like a good option. Again, our conclusion here is not that you are required to defer, only that it is OK to do so. Since you have a better route to the answer than thinking about it for yourself, it is OK not to think for yourself.

In addition to simply extending our arguments about deference more generally, it may be helpful to think about the role of moral advice and the process of moral education. As Sliwa (2012: 177) notes, relying on others for our moral beliefs is not an exotic phenomenon, it is something that is actually quite commonplace. It is hard to see how someone could become morally educated without heavily relying on the moral judgments of others. Further, self-aware individuals know that they are subject to biases and blindspots. Moral reasoning is particularly subject to such flaws in our thinking. However, once we recognize these limitations, our desire for the truth should lead us to seek moral advice from others.

While no one is entirely free of biases and blindspots, others typically don't share the very same biases and blindspots. If nothing else, the fact that they are not directly affected by the issue at hand can lend their judgments a greater degree of clarity. Thus, Sliwa (2012) argues that taking moral advice is good for two reasons:

> It's morally good because it helps us do the right thing in cases in which we might otherwise fail to do so. And it's epistemically good because it allows us to take advantage of our peers who may be epistemically better placed to make certain moral distinction and to come to the right moral conclusion. In short, we ask for and rely on moral advice because we're in many respects creatures who make mistakes, who get distracted, who are susceptible to biases, who have limited abilities of discrimination in some areas and who are, moreover, well aware of all that. Moral advice allows us to do the right thing despite all these limitations by tapping into the cognitive resources of our peers.
>
> (181)

For these reasons, moral advice seems perfectly appropriate, yet once we appreciate this fact, it is hard to see what could be wrong with moral deference. The reasons to take someone's moral advice carry over to taking their moral testimony and deferring. Recognizing that someone is in a better epistemic position to determine the answer to one's moral question gives them a reason to outsource that question.[26] Doing so gives them a better chance at getting to the truth than thinking about it for themselves.

THE UPSHOT

In this chapter we have examined a number of different proposals for treating deference in Socratic domains differently. While many cases of deference seem perfectly fine, many have found something problematic about deferring on matters of ethics, religion, politics, and philosophy more generally. The difficulty is in accounting for what, if anything, is different about these domains. Having explored several different rationales for treating these domains differently, we have not yet found any good reason to do so. Without such a reason, we should treat similar cases alike, and extend our central conclusion to these domains as well.

That said, the next two chapters can each be seen as extensions of this chapter. In Chapter 7 we will examine the vulnerability objection. According to the vulnerability objection, deference to the experts exacerbates our intellectual vulnerability. It may be thought that vulnerability in Socratic domains is particularly problematic. While we will simply examine the vulnerability objection across all domains, our discussion there can also be read as applying just to Socratic domains. In Chapter 8, we will explore the understanding objection. According to this objection, deference precludes understanding, and understanding is particularly valuable. Here too, it might be thought that understanding in Socratic domains is particularly important. While our discussion in Chapter 8 will examine this objection across all domains, this chapter too can be read as an extension of this current chapter with a focus on Socratic domains.[27]

Trust makes us vulnerable. If I trust you to pick me up from the airport, then I am at your mercy. If you don't show, I'm stuck. This is a kind of vulnerability that I don't have if I drive myself instead.[1] In not thinking for yourself, and outsourcing your intellectual projects to the relevant experts instead, you are made intellectually vulnerable. You are trusting the experts by taking them at their word, without seeing the reasons why they believe what they do. At the same time, experts are fallible. Experts have gotten it wrong. In addition, like the rest of us, experts can be biased, irresponsible, and even malicious. So, deference to the experts makes us intellectually vulnerable. Worse still, this vulnerability is not merely intellectual. How we act is based at least in part on our beliefs, so, when we are vulnerable in our beliefs, this vulnerability extends to our actions and to our lives more generally. For instance, my believing that you will pick me up, when you don't, doesn't just leave me with a false belief, it also leaves me stranded at the airport. In fact, I probably care a lot more about the effect of being stranded than I do about the fact that I now have one more false belief. Given all of this, it might look like not thinking for yourself is overly risky, that you are making yourself unnecessarily vulnerable, and that it is thereby problematic. According to the objection to be considered in this chapter, it is important that we think for ourselves in order to avoid this

DOI: 10.4324/9781003369004-8

kind of intellectual vulnerability. In thinking for ourselves, perhaps we can put an important check on the experts.

Having motivated this objection some more, I'll argue that in the end it fails. Intellectual vulnerability is simply inevitable for creatures like us. Such vulnerability is an ineliminable part of our intellectual lives. So, any hopes for intellectual invulnerability are bound to be disappointed. Further, while intellectual vulnerability is inevitable, relying on expert judgment actually *reduces* our vulnerability, rather than enhancing it. While checks and balances on expertise are no doubt important, I'll argue that thinking for yourself (as a non-expert) is not a good check on expertise. Rather, checks on expertise are more fruitfully done by other experts and on an institutional level.

MOTIVATING THE OBJECTION

"Because I said so." As a child, this parental response was never very satisfying. As children we wanted more of an explanation than that. We wanted *the reasons* why our parent said so, not just the fact that they did. We didn't want to be blind to their reasoning. The 'because I said so' explanation leaves open the possibility that there are no good reasons or that they have been mis-weighed. This lesson applies more generally. Believing merely on the basis of someone else's say-so leaves us vulnerable.

Deference leaves us both intellectually and practically vulnerable. Let's examine each type of vulnerability in turn. As Annette Baier (1986) has pointed out, our epistemic situation forces us to trust others, and trust makes us vulnerable. Thi Nguyen (2018b) expounds on this thought as follows: "When I trust a doctor, I make my body vulnerable; when I trust a romantic partner, I make my emotions vulnerable. When I trust another academic and rely on them, I make my belief system vulnerable." (115)

Further, the ever-increasing specialization, and hyperspecialization, in our society has only extended this vulnerability.[2] There are several ways in which deferring to the experts leaves us intellectually vulnerable. First, we can fail to get what we wanted. When deferring to an expert, we do so with certain expectations in hand. We come to them for the truth. We come to them for knowledge. That is what we expect from the expert, and if we don't get that, we are let down and our epistemic goals have been frustrated.

Second, in trusting an expert we can get what we *didn't* want; we can be misled. We don't go to experts to get false beliefs, yet in relying on their expertise, sometimes that is what we get. When we don't get to see the reasons on which the expert bases their belief, we are left to trust that they have correctly evaluated their evidence. We are taking them at their word. Further, we are trusting that their evidential basis is a good one. However, experts, despite their expertise, remain fallible thinkers. At different points in time, the relevant experts believed that the Earth was flat, that handwashing before a medical procedure wasn't important, that the atom was the smallest thing in the universe, that smoking didn't have any negative health outcomes, and many more claims that even small children today know to be false. Many of us are also aware of someone who has been misdiagnosed by their doctor. Even when the experts are doing their very best, they are working with finite minds, limited evidence, restricted time, and often tricky questions. Errors are to be expected. However, since experts, like us, are fallible thinkers, doesn't taking them at their word make us problematically vulnerable to their errors?

But, things get even worse. Not only can experts make mistakes, but there can also be bad players who intentionally deceive and are able to manipulate us due to the trust that we place in them.[3] The expert used car salesman may be in a far better epistemic position than you are regarding the quality of the cars on his lot, but his intentions are not always pure. He has an interest in making money, and often that interest is stronger than his interest in you having true beliefs about his cars.[4] If you merely trusted the used car salesman at his word, you would often be left worse off, both epistemically and financially.

This example leads us to the second way in which deferring to the experts leaves us vulnerable. Believing someone because they said so leaves us practically vulnerable as well. As DiPaolo (2022) puts it, "surrendering thinking often entails surrendering decision-making," and so, "practical dependence accompanies epistemic dependence." (236) When we make choices, our choices are informed by our beliefs, by our picture of what the world is like. So, when we trust others for our beliefs, their influence will often extend beyond our minds, and to our actions as well. For instance, suppose that your doctor tells you that you have cancer and that you need to undergo chemotherapy.[5] Since you are unable to assess the evidence and options for yourself, you believe the doctor at their word. In this case, the doctor's opinion influences not only your beliefs about the matter, but also the course of action that you take. Since you believe your doctor, you submit your body to the painful treatment that they recommend. If the doctor was mistaken in their diagnosis, the negative effects of your trust go well beyond your having a false belief. Your vulnerability here was not merely intellectual.

So, when experts are mistaken, the effects can often extend beyond the intellectual realm. Not only are you left with a false belief, often you will also be led on a course of action that you would not otherwise have undertaken. Further, just as you can be intellectually manipulated in your trust, you can also be practically manipulated. When you trust the car salesman, you don't just end up with a false belief, you also end up having paid more than you should have for a car that is less reliable than you believed.[6] The car salesman's goals are practical manipulation, it is just that the best way to get you to do what he wants is to get you to believe certain things first.

Given all of these risks, isn't it clear that individuals must think for themselves in order to avoid being taken advantage of in these ways? Doesn't our intellectual security demand it? Don't we need to think for ourselves to place an important check on expertise for our own intellectual, physical, and emotional well-being? That, at least, is what the vulnerability objection claims.

THE INEVITABILITY OF VULNERABILITY

What should we make of the vulnerability objection? The first layer of response to the vulnerability objection is to show how intellectual vulnerability is inevitable for creatures like us. According to Hardwig (1991: 693), trust is like the air we breathe. While it often goes unnoticed, it is absolutely essential for our lives. Put in the form of an SAT analogy, breathing is to life as trust is to knowledge. Hardwig continues as follows:

Modern knowers cannot be independent and self-reliant, not even in their own fields of specialization. In most disciplines, those who do not trust, cannot know; those who do not trust cannot have the best evidence for their beliefs. In an important sense, then, trust is often epistemologically more basic than empirical data or logical arguments.

(693–4)

Levy (2022b) notes several different ways in which trust is an inevitable part of even the researcher's life. First, research is often collaborative. Constraints on both time and specialization prevent researchers from being able to verify all of the claims of their collaborators. Second, trust is also required in principle as well. For instance, scientists must trust the instruments and tools that they use. They are typically not in a position to verify the reliability of these instruments for themselves. So, trust has an inevitable place in research.

However, even outside of active research, we must trust. The same considerations apply to us as laypeople who aren't on the front lines of research. Since trust is inevitable, vulnerability is also inescapable. It is now widely accepted in philosophy that the Cartesian epistemological project has failed. While Descartes sought to establish certainty for all of his beliefs, few think that we can be certain of much besides our own existence and perhaps our own mental states.[7] Rather, almost everything we know, or reasonably believe, we believe on the basis of *fallible reasons*. Fallible reasons are those that are compatible with the falsity of the belief in question. So, while I have good reason to believe that I have hands, all of my evidence for my having hands is consistent with my being a handless brain in a vat. I can't be *certain* that I am not a brain in a vat, even if I take myself to know things about the world around me. With uncertainty comes vulnerability, since uncertainty comes with the possibility of error. I can have strong reasons that you will pick me up from the airport, that I have beer in the fridge at home, that my car will start, and so forth, but in each case, my reasons are compatible with the falsity of those beliefs. My reasons can lead me astray. This isn't to say that they aren't still good reasons, just to note that even great reasons can let us down. While this may be an unfortunate feature of most of our reasons and beliefs, this is our intellectual lot in life. In addition to our reasons being fallible, we are also fallible thinkers. That is, we are also fallible in the way that we handle the reasons that we have. Sometimes we improperly ignore good reasons, other times we misevaluate the strength of some of our reasons. We don't always handle our reasons correctly. So, given the kind of creatures that we are, we are bound to a fate of epistemic vulnerability.

To be intellectually vulnerable, however, is not to be intellectually hopeless. Despite the fact that fallible reasons don't grant us certainty, our fallible reasons still serve us quite well. While there are no guarantees, and while things go wrong from time to time, in general, following our reasons helps us achieve our goals (intellectual and otherwise). It would be a mistake to think that uncertainty should lead us to give up on our intellectual pursuits. While we often cannot achieve certainty, we can still have better or worse reasons. In a world of uncertainty, it is not the case that anything goes. For instance, while certainty is off the table, there are still far better reasons to believe that humans are mammals, the Earth is quite old, and that Ottawa is the capital of Canada, than there are to believe their negations. We should still believe in line with our reasons even when our reasons don't guarantee the truth of the belief in question. The rational thing to do is to follow the evidence, even when the evidence offers no guarantees.[8] So, the inevitability of vulnerability does not give us a reason to quit our intellectual pursuits.

The same is true of our lives more generally. Our vulnerability extends beyond our intellectual lives. Everything about us is vulnerable. We are vulnerable to countless forces, both internal and external, that shape our lives. To take just one example, think of all the things that your health depends upon.

While there are things you can do to make yourself more, or less, healthy, whether you are successful in your pursuits depends upon internal and external forces that you simply cannot control. Whether you are even *alive* depends upon all sorts of factors that you cannot control. However, while there is nothing that we can do to make ourselves invulnerable, this doesn't mean that we should just give up. While we might see invulnerability as an ideal, it is simply not in the cards for creatures like us. But here too, this does not call for hopelessness. While there are no guarantees that your pursuits of health will succeed, this does not show that you shouldn't try.

So, while trusting others, and not thinking for yourself, leaves you intellectually vulnerable, it was an illusion to think that you were not intellectually vulnerable in the first place. There are simply no guarantees that come with thinking for yourself, except perhaps when thinking about your own existence. Thus, the fact that you are vulnerable when you trust others is not itself a reason not to do so. Vulnerability is simply inevitable.

That said, it is important to note that vulnerability comes in degrees. Vulnerability is not an all or nothing affair. So, while vulnerability may be inevitable, the *degree* to which we are vulnerable need not be. There are things that we can do that make ourselves more, or less, vulnerable. Having shelter, food, clothing, and so forth all makes us *less* vulnerable even if these things do not remove our vulnerability entirely. Further, playing with fire, juggling knives, and playing chicken with oncoming traffic are all activities that make us more vulnerable, even if we were bound to be vulnerable regardless. The same is true of our intellectual lives. Here too, while vulnerability is inevitable, we do have some degree of control over how vulnerable we are. So, we can reframe our vulnerability objection in light of this insight. Perhaps the problem here is not that trusting others makes us vulnerable full stop, but that it makes us *more* vulnerable or *excessively* vulnerable, and for that reason we should not do it; for that reason, it is important that we at least also think for ourselves. For instance, while we might be somewhat vulnerable every time we drive a car, when we outsource our intellectual projects, don't we negligently escalate our vulnerability? Isn't such intellectual outsourcing more like drunk driving – an unnecessary and negligent risk?

VULNERABILITY AND CHECKS & BALANCES

There are two things to say in response to this more sophisticated version of vulnerability objection. First, by deferring to experts we actually *decrease*, not increase, our intellectual vulnerability. Second, while it is important for there to be check and balances on the experts, appropriate checks don't come from thinking for yourself as a novice. Rather, effective checks on the experts should come from other experts or be conducted at the institutional level. Let's fill out both parts of this response in turn.

First, deference to the experts actually decreases our vulnerability. While we can't be certain of our conclusions, there are still better and worse ways of establishing them. While our reasons are often fallible reasons, we can still have better or worse reasons. Not all routes to the answers to our questions are equally good, even if all the available routes end with less than certain answers. This leads us back to thinking about expertise. Experts are those who are in a better epistemic position to answer our questions than we are (as non-experts). Experts have more, and better, evidence, and experts are better equipped to evaluate that evidence. In short, experts are more likely to uncover the answer. Again, even with experts there are no guarantees. So, in trusting the experts we remain vulnerable epistemic agents, but our vulnerability is decreased when we take better and more reliable routes to the answers.

So, relying on experts is a better route to the answers we seek than just thinking about things for ourselves, but isn't it better to *also* think things through for ourselves to better ensure that we are not being taken advantage of by the relevant experts? The problem with this line of thought is that since we lack the relevant expertise, thinking things through for ourselves won't be a helpful check on the experts. Recall that in Chapter 1 we saw that novices not only typically lack the experts' evidence, but were they to come to possess it, they would often be unable to understand it, or determine what it supports (and to what degree). Without the relevant training and expertise, we may be unable to understand the expert's reasons or be able to make any kind of determination about what they support.[9] Further, given our lack of expertise, our best attempts here are likely to only mislead us.[10] Given this, as novices we are often in no position to check or confirm the experts' claims.

While the novice can think about the claims of the expert, they should be hesitant to come to any conclusions on the basis of their own thinking about the matter. John Hardwig (1985) offers a similar caution as follows:

> This does not mean that [the novice] can never successfully raise a devastating objection to believing that p or imagine an alternative to believing that p, but it does mean that only someone with [the expert's] expertise can make an accurate assessment of the value and validity of the objection or alternative. Under cross-examination

by the layman, the expert may admit the cogency of a given point, but he (and his fellow experts) must judge whether it is cogent and germane, since they are the only ones who fully understand what is involved in the methods, techniques, premises, and bases of the expert's training and inquiry and how these affect the resultant belief.

(342)

Hardwig goes on to claim that "[r]ecognizing that the highest court of rational appeal lies outside of himself, the layman may simply have to accept the fact that his objection is not a good one, even though it still seems good to him." (342) As a novice, we may raise objections to expert opinion, and we may fail to understand or appreciate the expert's answers, but none of this means that we are thereby rational in rejecting the expert's verdict. We need to ask ourselves what best explains this state of affairs. It could be that we, as laypeople, have found a fatal flaw in the expert's reasoning or that the expert has failed to adequately appreciate some piece of evidence that we have correctly evaluated. However, given that they have the relevant expertise, and we do not, a far better explanation of this state of affairs is that our lack of expertise is preventing us from appreciating the evidence, or the expert's reasoning, correctly. For this reason, our thinking for ourselves about the matter will not be a good check on the experts. We are not rational in trusting our own evaluation of the evidence against that of the expert.

To further see this, let's consider a couple of examples. First, let's revisit our homeowner analogy. When Rico has an electrical issue and calls in the electrician, he is vulnerable. Of course, he is vulnerable regardless of whether he calls in the electrician. But, the electrician could misdiagnose the issue, or the electrician could intentionally deceive Rico and take advantage of him. In order to minimize his vulnerability, Rico could ask the electrician for the reasons why they came to the conclusion that they did regarding the needed electrical work. Rico could ask for an explanation. However, given that Rico is not himself an electrician, the explanation he then receives, and the reasons cited in favor of it, are likely to make little sense to Rico. For instance, the electrician might inform Rico that there is a problem with his residual current circuit breaker (RCCB) which is tripping due to an electrical current leak. Perhaps the electrician even shows Rico the RCCB so that Rico can examine it for himself. However, Rico has probably never seen an RCCB before, nor does he understand what he should even be looking for. His own examination of the relevant evidence is not going to provide any kind of reliable check on the electrician's claims. The electrician might tell him these things, but here too he is left trusting the electrician.

Second, let's consider a case of a medical diagnosis. Suppose that Than is getting ready to go to her annual physical. She has had some bloodwork done in advance, and the lab has just forwarded her the results. In looking over the results, Than notices that a couple of things are out of range. Seeing this, Than turns to the internet to google medical problems associated with the relevant abnormalities. She becomes convinced that she has a certain condition. When she goes in for her physical, Than's doctor explains that the reference ranges only cover what is typical for about 95% of the population. Given Than's particular medical history, it was to be expected that she fell out of range on these items. The doctor explains that there is no health issue or concern here. Than should believe her doctor. Her doctor is far better equipped to make these judgments, and her self-diagnosis is not an effective check on a doctor's diagnosis.[11]

What these examples show is that thinking for yourself is not a reliable check on expert opinion. However, this is not to say that there is nothing else you can do, or that there shouldn't be any checks on expert opinion. When the stakes are high enough, you don't want to simply take a solitary expert at their word. If the solution isn't to think for yourself, then what is it? For all the same reasons that we have discussed, here too you should rely on the experts. When Rico receives the report from the electrician, his thinking for himself about the matter isn't going to place a reliable check on the electrician's diagnosis, but, calling in a second electrician would offer such a check. When Than receives her diagnosis from her doctor, thinking for herself about the relevant reasons won't reduce Than's vulnerability. If anything, it will only increase it. The way to reduce her vulnerability is to get a second opinion from another medical professional. Importantly, not all second opinions are equally worthwhile. It is a second opinion from an expert that will reduce Than's vulnerability, not her own opinion. Rather, it is relying on other experts that can place a valuable check on expert opinion.

THE IMPORTANCE OF INSTITUTIONS

Before moving on, it is worth addressing a particularly troubling way in which our intellectual vulnerability can be exploited. In doing so, we can see one further layer of defense that we can have against expertise gone awry. Larry Nassar was a long-time team doctor for USA Gymnastics. For decades Nassar deceived and sexually assaulted hundreds of female athletes under the guise of professional medical treatment. Nassar used his medical expertise to deceive athletes into believing that they were receiving legitimate medical treatment and to conceal his abuse. The cover that his expertise provided allowed him to abuse hundreds of individuals over many years. Nassar is an example of what Lackey (2021b) calls a 'predatory expert.' Predatory experts are experts who use their epistemic authority to hide their predatory behavior. (144) In short, predatory experts abuse the trust placed in them to manipulate others, they exploit the vulnerability of those who trust them.

The existence of predatory experts raises a further challenge to our central conclusion.[12] According to our central conclusion, it is OK not to think for yourself. After all, there is typically someone who is better suited to answer your question for you. In the case of Nassar, we have a medical professional. Medical professionals are better suited to answer questions related to their expertise than laypeople are. Given this, it was rational for these athletes to trust their doctor. Their doctor, however, abused this trust and used it to manipulate, exploit, and assault these individuals. The athletes in question used their reasons to trust their doctor to suppress their own concerns over the 'treatments' they were receiving. Trusting the relevant expert only perpetuated the problem. Clearly things have gone wrong in cases of predatory experts like this. The question is how do we best prevent such cases of abuse?

One possible response is to advocate for more thinking for yourself. According to this line of thought, if people thought more for themselves, they would be less vulnerable to predatory experts like Nassar. As we have seen, though, there are good reasons to doubt the novice's ability to check the expert's expertise. In addition, this response seemingly also has the result that the victims of such sexual assault were being irrational or irresponsible. If their own reasons where indeed better or stronger reasons than those offered by the relevant expert, then the rational thing for them to believe was in line with their own reasons. But, such a response places blame on the wrong party, it blames the victim. It claims that their assault was the result of their own irrationality (at least in part). This is a mistake. Unfortunately, part of what makes cases of exploitation like this possible is that the individual in question can be correctly following their evidence. The failures here were not failures of individual rationality or cases of intellectual irresponsibility. Rather, the failures here were institutional. Nassar's abuse was able to go on for so long because there were not appropriate institutional safeguards in place. What this means is that the appropriate checks and balances on authority don't come from within the (novice) individual. Rather, the way to address such abuse and work to prevent their reoccurrence comes at the institutional level.[13]

In fact, this is precisely how USA Gymnastics has responded to the scandal. One of the changes made by USA Gymnastics in response to the scandal is that all USA Gymnastics members are now required to report *any* suspected sexual misconduct to the relevant authorities. Importantly, this is *not* a requirement that one must first be reasonable in believing that there is sexual misconduct before reporting. *Any* suspicion or uneasiness must be reported to the relevant parties, regardless of whether one has sufficient reasons to believe that abuse has in fact happened. In doing so, the institution can better identify abuse, and patterns of abuse, in ways that no one individual could. In addition, reports are made anonymously, so the fear of backlash does not suppress reports of potential abuse. Increased education has also been a focus for parents, clubs, and individual athletes. However, while there is a role for increased education, the fact remains that significant power (and knowledge) differentials create the potential for rational manipulation. As such, institutions must play an important role in protecting individuals.

Javier González de Prado has made similar points concerning the phenomenon of gaslighting.[14] Gaslighting occurs when an individual is given misleading doubts about their own epistemic abilities. It is a kind of psychological manipulation where one is left questioning their own intellectual credentials or competence. Gaslighting typically occurs when an individual, the gaslighter, has (or is at least perceived to have) epistemic authority over the victim of their manipulation. Gaslighting undermines the victim's ability to use their own reasons, or to rely on their own weighing of the reasons, given the self-doubts that have been created by the gaslighter. As Abramson (2014) has put it, gaslighting is an attempt to make the victim lose their "independent standing as deliberator." (8) However, gaslighting does not only succeed when the victim is being irrational. Unfortunately, gaslighting often works because the victim is *correctly* following their reasons. As González de Prado (2021) claims, "Gaslighting has the perverse feature that it achieves its harmful effects via the autonomous responses of the victim. In a sense, the victim autonomously collaborates with the undoing of her own autonomy." (265)[15]

As we have seen, rationality does not come with invulnerability. Here too, one can correctly follow their reasons yet be manipulated in so doing.[16] So, for similar reasons, defenses to gaslighting do not consist of simply taking more care to evaluate one's own reasons. Often it is the very evaluation of these reasons that lead to the manipulation. Here too, our best defenses lie outside of our own thinking.[17]

This lesson here applies more broadly as well. Verifying information from experts is simply too much work for any one individual to do, even if they were capable of doing so. So, we need institutions that we can rely on to provide such checks and to better secure our safety. For instance, food and drug manufacturers make claims about what their products contain and what possible effects they might have. Verifying these claims would be too difficult, and too much work, for any individual to do. However, we aren't stuck with blind faith in food and drug manufacturers. In this case, we have an institution, the FDA (the US Food and Drug Administration), that monitors and verifies the claims made by such manufacturers. The FDA acts as an important check on these authoritative claims that individuals are simply unable to do.

Such a picture shifts the focus of our trust from individuals to institutions. As philosophers Gernot Rieder and Judith Simon (2016) explain this change:

> The veracity of testimony was no longer underwritten by personal virtue, but by an elaborate system of institutionalized norms and standards, rigorously policed in a great "panopticon of truth" (Shapin, 1994). A different form of trust first accompanied and then superseded the premoderns' faith in the integrity of the solitary knower and the moderns' confidence in the rigor of institutionalized expertise.
>
> (3)

So, in our specialized society, it is important for us to rely on what Grasswick (2020: 177) calls "a vast array of already functioning social practices that embody networks of epistemic trust in inquiry and testimony." Such institutional safeguards help to ensure that we can better function as epistemic agents and as people more generally.[18] Here is how Levy (2022a) puts it:

> We can't have any guarantees. The epistemic condition, for beings like us who are pervasively dependent on distributed cognition and specialized inquiry, is to rely on institutions and individuals to perform their tasks sufficiently well for reliability. We have to trust them: not in their good will (some will certainly fail to exhibit it), but for the proper functioning of the multiple mechanisms that promote error correction, the cancelling out of bias and the eventual identification of corruption. The history of science seems to indicate that for the most part, however, these mechanisms work sufficiently well most of the time. So the experts tell me, and I believe them.
>
> (356)

THE UPSHOT

In this chapter we have examined the vulnerability objection to our central conclusion. According to this objection, deferring to others leaves us too vulnerable, and this vulnerability is best addressed by thinking for yourself. In response we have seen that we need to abandon any illusions of the possibility of intellectual invulnerability. Creatures like us cannot avoid being vulnerable. While it is valuable to minimize our vulnerability, we have seen that thinking for yourself, when you are not an expert yourself, is not a promising way of doing so. While expertise should not go unchecked, it is better checked by other experts and by institutions.

So, thinking for yourself does not offer an escape from intellectual vulnerability. In the next chapter we will look at something else that thinking for yourself offers – understanding. According to the understanding objection, understanding is an epistemically valuable state, and it is something that you can only achieve if you think for yourself. Given this, it is argued that we have a strong reason to think for ourselves.

The Understanding Objection

We are all after epistemic improvement. We want true beliefs. We want to move from true beliefs to knowledge. And we want to move from knowledge to understanding. Understanding is perhaps the highest intellectual good. At the same time, understanding seems to require doing the intellectual work yourself. You can't understand the answer to your question when you believe it just because someone else said so. This seems to raise a problem for our central conclusion. If deference robs us of understanding, it looks like we have a strong reason *not* to defer – a powerful reason to think for ourselves. In brief, the objection goes like this: understanding is more valuable than knowledge, yet understanding can only be obtained when an individual thinks for themselves. You cannot gain understanding by deference. So, people should think for themselves so that they can obtain this state of greater epistemic value – so that they can understand.

Having motivated the objection some more, I'll agree with much of what it claims. I'll agree that understanding is more valuable than knowledge, and I'll agree that understanding comes only by way of thinking for yourself. What I'll reject is the idea that we must always go for the best. While understanding is better than knowledge, having knowledge is often good enough. So long as knowledge is good enough, it is OK to not do more and strive for an even

DOI: 10.4324/9781003369004-9

more valuable epistemic state. Given this, it is OK not to think for yourself.

MOTIVATING THE OBJECTION

Before we look at what deference can't do, let's first recap what it *can* do. When you defer to an expert you can come to have a true belief. When you believe what they say, if what they say is true, then you thereby come to have a true belief. For your belief to be true, you don't need to possess any reasons whatsoever, your belief simply must match reality. But, deferring to an expert can give you more. As we have seen in the first two chapters, deference to the experts can give you a rational belief. When you defer, you believe on the basis of someone else's say-so. In doing so, you don't get their reasons (the direct reasons) for their belief. However, as we have seen, you can have good reason to believe that they have good reasons for their belief (indirect reasons). When you have good reason to believe that someone is an expert, you have good reason to believe that their beliefs about matters in their area of expertise are well supported. After all, experts have superior bodies of evidence and are especially capable of evaluating such evidence. So, when you find out that an expert has a certain belief about a matter of their expertise, you have reason to believe that they have significant evidence that they have correctly evaluated to support that belief. We called these reasons to believe that someone else has reasons 'indirect reasons,' and we saw in Chapter 1 that it can be reasonable to believe things on the basis of indirect reasons alone. So, in deferring to the experts you can come to have a reasonable belief in addition to a true belief. On top of this, you can even come to have knowledge on the basis of deference to the experts. What exactly it takes to have knowledge is itself a contentious philosophical question, but on many accounts, knowledge requires at least having a reasonable, true belief. While there is no consensus account of knowledge, pretty much everyone agrees that we can gain knowledge by way of testimony. So, truth, rationality, and knowledge are all possible epistemic goods that we can gain through deference.

What the objection on offer here claims is that there is more to be had than truth, rationality, and knowledge. The epistemic good that is beyond all of these is understanding.

What is understanding? Well, here too there is nothing like a philosophical consensus, but there are several common features that we can point to. Following Elgin (2007) we can see that understanding is a kind of epistemic success that can vary along three main dimensions: breadth, depth, and significance. You have a *broader* understanding of a proposition when you can fit this belief into a more comprehensive system of beliefs, when there are more connections to other beliefs that you have. You have a *deeper* understanding of a proposition when the connections between this belief and others are less superficial, and the connections are tighter. The depth of understanding concerns the strength of the connections to other beliefs, and their degree of fit. Finally, you have a more *significant* understanding of a proposition when you recognize not only its truth but also its significance and relevance.[1] In all of these ways, understanding involves a kind of cognitive integration. When one understands, they see how things fit together, and the result is a better picture of reality.

What is the value of understanding?[2] To start, understanding seems to be something that we simply want. As Hazlett (2016) puts it, "Even when some proposition is well supported by testimonial evidence, many people still want to understand the (non-testimonial) argument that supports it, to grasp the (non-testimonial) evidence for it, or to see it for themselves." (131)

Jager (2016) similarly argues that subjects don't just want true beliefs. Rather, what a subject wants is to enhance their understanding by "grasping systematic connections among elements of a complex whole, or gaining insight into certain relations between items within a larger body of information." (180) On this picture, understanding is subjectively satisfying. Understanding appeases our curiosity in ways that mere knowledge does not.[3] Someone who understands has completed the mental puzzle – they have put the pieces together, and that comes with a kind of satisfaction.

Others have seen the value of understanding as residing in the fact that understanding gives us a better cognitive reflection of reality. While true beliefs, rational beliefs, and knowledge all entail a kind of correspondence between one's mind and the world, understanding comes with a fuller picture of the world. The mind/world connection is richer with understanding than it is with knowledge, rational beliefs, or merely true beliefs. Since our intellectual goal is to reflect reality in our minds, understanding best satisfies our intellectual goals.

The benefits here are also not merely intellectual. Understanding, by giving us a better picture of the world, increases our ability to successfully navigate the world. With this richer cognitive picture of the world in hand, those who understand are better equipped to predict and control the world around them.[4] Appreciating the connections between various truths allows us to better make things happen in the world. For instance, if I understand a law of nature, rather than simply knowing that it is true, I am better able to both predict what will happen and control what happens. So, understanding comes with practical benefits as well.

Still others have seen the value of understanding as a special kind of intellectual achievement. Along these lines, Pritchard (2016) takes 'seeing it for oneself' as a strong cognitive achievement and the ultimate goal of inquiry. When one understands, success is primarily attributable to the agent themself. This differs from mere knowledge, because when I come to know via testimony, the resulting knowledge is often not to my credit. The hard intellectual work was done by the testifier. For instance, it is one thing to give a friend a cake, it is another to bake them a cake. If I come to understand an answer, there is some cognitive success that I have achieved. I've put the pieces together and grasped the answer. No one can do that for me. Further, such achievements are valuable in and of themselves – they have what philosophers call final value.

These considerations about the value of understanding also point to its connection with thinking for yourself. Before thinking about understanding more generally, let's first look at what has been said about the connection between moral understanding and thinking for yourself.[5] Hills (2009) claims the following:

> If you understand why X is morally right or wrong, you must have some appreciation of the reasons why it is wrong. Appreciating the reasons why it is wrong is not the same as simply believing that they are the reasons why it is wrong, or even knowing that they are the reasons why it is wrong. Moral understanding involves a grasp of the relation between a moral proposition and the reasons why it is true.
>
> (101)

Here, having the direct reasons for the belief in question is essential for understanding it. You cannot understand the answer if you don't possess the reasons that directly support it. Since deference involves not getting the direct reasons for the belief, but rather simply believing on someone else's say-so, deference seems to preclude understanding. While Hills' focus is moral understanding, this conclusion extends beyond the moral case to understanding more generally. Zagzebski (2008) claims the following regarding the relationship between understanding and thinking for yourself: "understanding cannot be given to another person at all except in the indirect sense that a good teacher can sometimes recreate the conditions that produce understanding in hopes that the student will acquire it also." (146)

Here, the idea is that understanding essentially involves appreciating the relevant reasons for oneself. While this can occur with the help of another, it cannot simply be given to someone through testimony. While someone can help you understand, they cannot simply give you understanding. In order to understand, you need to put the work in yourself. Understanding requires having the direct reasons.

Let's turn to some examples to further motivate the point. When I first heard that $10 = 9.\overline{99}$, I was incredulous. The claim seemed obviously false to me. After all, one number had a tens digit and the other did not. How could they possibly be equivalent? However, I was told of this equivalence by a trusted mathematician, so I believed them. In believing my mathematician friend, I came to know that 10 is equivalent to $9.\overline{99}$ (it really is true!), but I still didn't get it. I didn't grasp its truth. I was unsatisfied with just trusting my friend, so he sent me some videos that explained this mathematical truth. For instance, if you take 10 and divide it by 3, you will get $3.\overline{33}$. That is easy to see. However, if you then take that result, $3.\overline{33}$, and multiply it by 3, you get $9.\overline{99}$. However, when you divide a number by three, and then multiply that quotient by 3, you should arrive back at where you started. Dividing and then multiplying by the same number will bring you full circle. So, it follows that $10 = 9.\overline{99}$. Thinking things through in this way helped me to see this mathematical truth for myself. I now understood it, whereas before I simply knew it on the basis of my friend's testimony. Where I arrived after thinking about it for myself was an intellectually more valuable place to be and I only got there by engaging the reasoning for myself.

Logic puzzles also present good examples here. A few years ago, there was a riddle circulating the internet: If Theresa's daughter is my daughter's mother, then what am I to Theresa? Here are the possible answers: a) I am her Grandmother, b) I am her Mother, c) I am her Daughter, d) Granddaughter, e) I am Theresa. Go ahead and think about it for a second, since it is more fun to think about these things without first knowing the answer. The answer is in this next footnote.[6]

It is one thing to know what the answer is, and it is another thing to see it for yourself – to grasp its truth, to understand it. Here's how to do that if you haven't yet succeeded. Replace 'my daughter's mother' with 'me.' Since all the possible answers are female, we know that I must be female, and so I must be my daughter's mother. If I am female, then my daughter's mother is just myself. Replacing the original prompt with this equivalent phrase we get 'If Theresa's daughter is me, then what am I to Theresa?' Now it is quite simple. Clearly, I am Theresa's daughter. If things went well for you, you now see it for yourself. You understand the answer, and that is of greater epistemic value. Things have improved from when you simply knew the answer.

In both of these cases, we can see that people can come to be in an improved epistemic position toward the answer by thinking about it for themselves. Sure, they could have had a true belief, a reasonable belief, and even knowledge just by deferring to the right person, but in gathering the relevant direct reasons and evaluating them for themselves, they came to have something that is even better – they came to understand the answer. So, you have a strong epistemic reason to think for yourself. In thinking for yourself you can come to grasp the answer, to understand it, and that is more valuable than merely knowing it. Further, this valuable state is simply not one that you can achieve by deferring to someone else. In order to understand the answer, you need to engage with the reasons yourself. So, in not thinking for yourself you are settling for a sub-optimal epistemic state. You are required to think for yourself so that you can meet your fullest potential – you can do better.

That's the understanding objection to our central conclusion. What can be said in response? In what follows we will explore two responses to the understanding objection. The first claims that understanding actually can be transmitted via testimony, so deference does not in fact block us from obtaining understanding. The second grants that understanding cannot be gained by testimony and that understanding is of greater epistemic value than knowledge, but argues that nevertheless it is OK to defer. It remains OK to defer since it is OK to do less than one's best so long as the alternative is good enough.

UNDERSTANDING WITHOUT THINKING FOR YOURSELF

One way to respond to the understanding objection is to reject the link between understanding and thinking for yourself. According to this line of thought, understanding *can* be had even when one defers. How might understanding be transmitted via deference? Here we will look at two different proposals. According to the first, understanding just is a certain kind of knowledge, so since knowledge can be transmitted through deference, so too can understanding. The second claims that while understanding involves more than knowledge, sometimes the extra bit is so easy to come by that we can see it as coming with the knowledge through testimony.

Some philosophers have seen understanding as a kind of knowledge. For instance, Sliwa (2015) defends a reductionist view of understanding according to which knowledge is both necessary and sufficient for understanding. On this account, an individual understands why a proposition is true just in case they know why it is true, and they understand *that* proposition just in case they know that proposition.[7] So, since knowledge can be transmitted via testimony, so too can understanding. Nothing else is needed. On this picture of understanding, then, the understanding objection simply fails to gain any traction.

However, there is reason to require more for understanding the answer than for knowing the answer. Knowing the answer doesn't require grasping it or seeing it for yourself, as understanding does.[8] As Kvanvig (2003) claims, "What is distinctive about understanding … is the internal seeing or appreciating of explanatory and other coherence inducing relationships in a body of information that is crucial for understanding." (198) For instance, an individual can know why something is true, since they can parrot back the reasoning that they have been told, but this is importantly different than them seeing why those are good reasons. Understanding requires the appreciation of those connections as opposed to simply knowing that they are there. So, this first response to the understanding objection fails.

A second response argues that while understanding is distinct from knowledge, it nevertheless can be transmitted via testimony. For instance, Boyd (2017) has argued that testimony does not preclude understanding. If he is right, then the understanding objection loses its bite. Boyd sees understanding as consisting of two components: the informational component and the grasping component. When you understand a proposition, you have the reasons, and you see why they support the belief in question. This is why it might be thought that you cannot gain understanding by testimony. While testimony can transmit the information, you cannot transmit the grasping, or the requisite abilities to grasp the reasons, by testimony.

To address this issue, Boyd distinguishes between two kinds of understanding: easy and difficult. Difficult understanding occurs when the information itself doesn't easily lend itself to being grasped. Grasping, in difficult cases, takes a great deal of effort, time, and ability on the part of the hearer. However, in cases of easy understanding, the grasping comes from simply comprehending the information that is being transmitted. So, while only the information can be transmitted in testimony, in cases of easy understanding, receiving the information is sufficient for the grasping of it as well. This is how understanding can be transmitted through testimony.

Whether Boyd is correct or not, his argument fails to apply to the type of cases that concern us here. The cases under consideration here are those of deference, where the subject believes the expert simply on the basis of their say-so. In cases of deference, the speaker is not giving the hearer their reasons (the direct reasons) for the belief in question. So, even if understanding could be given by way of testimony if the direct reasons were shared (since grasping them is sufficiently easy), these are not the cases that concern us here.

Boyd's cases are those where thinking for yourself about the matter is very easily done. But they are cases where the subject is still doing some thinking for themselves. In particular, they are cases where the subject is receiving and evaluating the relevant direct reasons on their own. So, the cases where Boyd thinks that understanding is transmitted through testimony are not the kind of cases relevant to our discussion. In the cases relevant to our central conclusion, the direct reasons remain foreign to the hearer.[9] So, both attempts to reconcile understanding and testimony fail, at least for our purposes here. We will need to look elsewhere for a response to the understanding objection.

SETTING THE SCOPE

Before turning to our second line of defense to the understanding objection, it is worth clarifying the scope of the objection. Even if the objection is fully successful, it will not follow that we should *always* or even *often* think for ourselves. The reason is that understanding isn't always on the table. In cases where thinking for yourself wouldn't result in understanding, you are still without reason to think for yourself. Understanding might be unavailable for several reasons. First, it could be that no one understands the answer, perhaps no one even knows the answer. For instance, consider questions that are at, or beyond, the boundaries of human knowledge: How many species are there? Is there life on other planets? Why do we have an appendix? In addition, consider contentious questions about the nature of the quantum world, the nature of personal identity, or the fairest system of taxation. Even if you thought long and hard about these questions, you wouldn't come away understanding the answers. The reason why is that *no one* understands the answers to these questions!

At least not yet. Not even the experts have been able to settle these questions, so your novice inquiry won't end with you understanding the answer. Even if you happened on the right answer, the fact that the relevant debate is in a state of disarray would prevent you from even having a rational belief about it.[10] So, some questions are such that understanding the answer simply isn't an option. But, if you are not going to understand the answer, then you would lose your reason to think for yourself. In such cases, you can know that the potential epistemic gains simply aren't there to be had.

Second, even in cases where understanding is possible, there is no guarantee that you will get it. In many cases, thinking for yourself will be unlikely to deliver understanding even if understanding is there to be had. Recall Boyd's distinction between easy and difficult cases of understanding. Some things are simply hard to understand. Einstein allegedly claimed that income tax was the hardest thing to understand. Thinking long and hard about many questions does not guarantee that you will understand the answer. Further, understanding the answer may require that you develop certain skills, learn key concepts, and become aware of a great deal of background information. All of that can take significant time and energy. For instance, there are many mathematical theorems that I don't think I would come to understand even if I gave them my very best efforts. So, some questions have answers that may be too difficult for us to understand. Alternatively, it may simply be quite unlikely that we will understand the answer. If the potential reward is very unlikely, then even if it is possible, it seems like we would lose our reason to think for ourselves.

Finally, there is the issue of our finitude. Even if we could understand everything that we put our minds to, we can only put our minds to so much. The time and effort that would go into understanding one answer, is time and effort that could not go to understanding some other answer. Since our time and effort are both limited, our opportunities for understanding are also limited. What this means is that even if the understanding objection was fully successful, it would only show that there are some occasions where we should think for ourselves. As such, it is a much more modest objection to our central conclusion. However, even with its more limited scope in mind, I think that there are reasons to resist the understanding objection.

EPISTEMIC SATISFICING

So, let's grant that understanding is more valuable than knowledge and that it can only come by way of thinking for yourself. Does it follow that we should think for ourselves? Does it follow that we are *required* to? In order for our central conclusion to be false, it would need to be the case that we have a requirement to think for ourselves, an intellectual obligation to do so, that it would be wrong not to. If deferring does not violate any intellectual rule or duty, then it would still be OK not to think for yourself. Given that understanding is more valuable than anything that we can get by way of deference and that understanding only comes by thinking for yourself, the issue comes down to whether we need to do our intellectual best – whether we need to be epistemic maximizers. Are we required to aim for, or achieve, the highest possible epistemic state that we can, or is it fine for us to do less than our intellectual best? In what follows, I will make the case that it is perfectly fine for us to do less than our best; some epistemic states are good enough, even though they could be improved upon. For this reason, I'll argue that it remains OK not to think for yourself.

Before defending this answer, however, let's look at the parallel question in the domain of morality. When it comes to ethics, there are a number of different theories about what makes the right actions right, and what makes the wrong actions wrong. These are central questions in normative ethics. Another related issue in normative ethics is whether it is morally permissible to do less than the best. Put differently, the issue is whether some actions are above and beyond the moral call of duty. Actions that are above and beyond the call of duty are called 'supererogatory actions.' Supererogatory moral actions come with greater moral value, but they are not actions that we are morally required to do. For instance, suppose that a soldier is in a bunker with several fellow soldiers. Unfortunately, a grenade falls into the bunker. There are only moments to act. Our soldier could try to get as far away as possible from the grenade or find something to shelter himself from the explosion. However, yet another option is for the soldier to jump on the grenade and thereby sacrifice himself while protecting his fellow soldiers from the explosion. Many ethicists see this last alternative as supererogatory. If the soldier chooses to sacrifice his life to save his fellow soldiers, he does something that goes above and beyond the call of duty. If he had instead sought his own shelter, this would have also been a morally permissible action. So, his sacrifice wasn't something that was morally required of him. Further, his sacrifice was a morally better option. His action brings about a state of greater moral value, more lives were saved as a result of his sacrifice. So, his action was better than it needed to be; morality did not demand it of him.

To use a less gruesome example, we can consider an individual who takes on a second job in order to earn some more money. They take on this second job for the purpose of donating all of the resulting income to a worthwhile charity. In doing so, they add a number of working hours to their week, all so that they can do more to help those in need. Such an individual should be commended for their actions. What they did was morally praiseworthy, it was better that they did this as opposed to simply enjoying more time relaxing, but this wasn't something that was morally required of them. They went above and beyond the moral call of duty in an admirable way. Individuals who don't get a second job to donate the extra earnings to charity do not thereby do something morally wrong. Having just one job and giving a portion of your income to charity is plausibly a good enough way to live your life; such a life fulfills the moral requirements. For instance, it would be inappropriate to blame people for not taking on this noble endeavor of taking on a second job for the sake of charitable giving. So, here too we have an instance of a morally good (or better) action that is nevertheless not a moral requirement.

What the existence of such morally supererogatory acts shows us is that we are not always morally required to do the very best thing that we can do. All that morality requires is that we perform an action, or live a life, that is good enough. When you go for an option that is good enough, though not optimal, you satisfice. Moral satisficing occurs when individuals act in morally good enough ways, even though they could have acted in even better ways. For instance, giving 20% of your paycheck to charity is plausibly a good enough way to live your life, even though it remains true that you could have done something even better.[11] For instance, you could have given more money and thereby done more good. Even though there was a morally better option for you to take, you weren't morally required to do it. We aren't all required to be moral saints or heroes.

Let's return to the intellectual realm with the concepts of supererogation and satisficing in hand. What we've seen so far is that understanding is more epistemically valuable than knowledge. We are also taking for granted that understanding can only be achieved by thinking for yourself; by acquiring, evaluating, and appreciating the relevant direct reasons for yourself. The value of understanding clearly gives you a reason to think for yourself. By so doing, you can bring about a better epistemic state in yourself. But does the possibility of a better epistemic state also *require* that you think for yourself? There is a requirement to think for yourself only if knowledge, or the other goods that can be gained by deference, are not good enough on their own. My argument is that knowledge typically is good enough. If knowledge is good enough, then thinking for yourself would not be required. Even if understanding is a more valuable state, it would be supererogatory to obtain it.[12] In other words, thinking for yourself would be going above and beyond the intellectual call of duty. Something that is fine and good to do, but not something that you *must* do.

To motivate the idea that some epistemic states are good enough, even though they could be improved upon, consider the following case from Hedberg (2014).[13] Imagine an individual who, at the end of the day, takes an intellectual inventory of all of the small and subtle beliefs that they have subconsciously picked up throughout the day. Beliefs about why a co-worker left early, about the moods of various people they passed in traffic, and other beliefs that were likely brought about by heuristics and other mental shortcuts they subconsciously took throughout the day. Bringing these beliefs to mind, our subject more carefully scrutinizes their evidential bases, discarding those beliefs that snuck in without sufficient evidential support. Such critical reflection on mundane everyday beliefs is laudable, but it is also unnecessary. As Tidman (1996) puts it,

> Even the most diligent knowers fail to critically reflect upon the bulk of their ordinary day-to-day beliefs. Indeed, it is pretty easy to produce a shopping list of ordinary beliefs one has never even noticed, much less critically reflected upon.
>
> (269)

While the result of such critical reflection is an improved intellectual state, it is too demanding to expect everyone to take such rigorous care of their doxastic lives. So, one does not violate any intellectual rules or duties by failing to do so. Even if such careful reflection is to be commended, it is perfectly fine not to engage in such an intellectual exercise even if it does bring about epistemic improvements.

To take another case, consider my writing of this book.[14] In preparing to write this book, I did a lot of research. I read a number of books, countless papers, and engaged in many conversations with fellow philosophers. Each paper I read would point me to at least two or three other papers that had some connection to the topic at hand. The research process could have been endless. No doubt, with every new paper I could read, I could thereby have improved my intellectual state. The intellectual foundation for this project would have been ever improved by reading an ever-increasing amount of work. However, no one can read everything. At some point you have to decide that you have read enough for the project, or else the project would never get off the ground. Some amount of research is good enough, even though you could always do more and things could always get better. So, here too we can see that sometimes an intellectual state is good enough, even though it can be improved upon.

The permissibility of satisficing is particularly plausible when there is no maximal state to obtain. If you could *always* do better, not doing the best that you could ceases to be a criticism that has any bite. What is important in such cases is that you do good enough. For instance, I often tell my students that a paper can always get better, that it is never the best that it can be. Their job is to make their paper as good as they can before the deadline. Often the resulting papers are good enough, even if they always could be better still. Epistemically, we can always do better. We can always gather more evidence, run more tests, double and triple-check the results, and so forth. In improving our evidential base, we can become even more reasonable in our beliefs, and we can build an evidential base that is even more resilient to potential defeaters. Both are valuable intellectual improvements. Further, we can always be training our minds, improving in intellectual virtue, and spending more time thinking about matters in order to better ensure that we have evaluated our evidence correctly. So, our evidence can always improve, and our ability to evaluate it correctly can always improve as well. Our epistemic position is one that can always get better. That said, we do not thereby flout some intellectual rule by failing to continuously do so. Regarding many propositions, our epistemic state is good enough as it is. Further improvements are simply unnecessary even if they are valuable improvements. It is fine (and even praiseworthy) to do so, if you so choose, but it is not a requirement of rationality.

For instance, I know that Washington was the first US president, that Canada is the country with the second largest landmass, and that every even number is divisible by two. In fact,

I take myself to be quite epistemically well-positioned with respect to each of these truths. However, I could nevertheless perpetually improve my epistemic position regarding each of these claims. There are people whose epistemic position regarding these claims is even better than mine. They have more and even better evidence, and their intellectual faculties are superior to mine. However, I don't think that any of this requires that I continually be working to improve my epistemic state regarding these claims. Not only do I have a good epistemic position regarding them, but my epistemic position is quite good, and it is certainly good enough. Gathering yet more evidence here would be going above and beyond my epistemic duties. It is simply not necessary. It is perfectly OK for me not to do so, even though epistemic improvement is still possible.

So, how does all of this apply to the understanding objection? In deferring to the experts, you do not allow yourself to come to understand the answer to your question. So, in not thinking for yourself, you are settling for a sub-optimal epistemic state – something short of understanding. However, while deference can't get you understanding, it can get you some very valuable epistemic goods. Recall that deference can get you a true belief, a rational belief, and even knowledge. In what follows, we will focus on knowledge, since knowledge is the strongest epistemic state that one can get from deference. Our response claims that even if understanding is more valuable than knowledge, knowledge is still quite valuable. Further, knowledge is often good enough, and so we are not required to go for more.

What's so special about knowledge? Aristotle begins *The Metaphysics* by claiming that everyone by nature desires knowledge. A common view in epistemology is that knowledge is the goal of inquiry.[15] Inquiring minds want to know. In other words, when we inquire into a question, we want to settle that question, and we can settle that question by knowing the answer. Inquirers care about knowledge because knowledge satisfies their concern for truth.[16] Once we know the answer to our question, further inquiry is superfluous.[17]

This is not to say it would be wrong to continue inquiry. In fact, it might be the case that it is sometimes better to do so. In striving for understanding one might act as an epistemological saint or hero. Doing so may be praiseworthy, but it is not required. We are permitted to stop our inquiry when we have something that is good enough, and often that is knowledge.

Returning to previous examples, you may want to understand why $10 = 9.\overline{99}$, why the answer is c) I am Theresa's daughter, or why this road is the road to Larissa. If so, then thinking about it for yourself is the way to go. If you want to understand these answers, you will need to acquire and evaluate the evidence for yourself. In doing so, you may achieve understanding and thereby come to be in a better epistemic state. However, you may instead have been satisfied with just knowing what the relevant answers are — knowing that $10 = 9.\overline{99}$, knowing that the answer was c), and knowing that this is the road to Larissa. If so, then I think that is perfectly OK too. Coming to know the answer to your question is good enough. There is no rational requirement to also understand the answer. Knowing is good enough, and it is something that you can get without thinking for yourself. So, the understanding objection fails.[18]

THE UPSHOT

This chapter has been concerned with the understanding objection. According to this objection, individuals are required to think for themselves so that they can achieve the more valuable state of understanding – a state that is only available to those who think for themselves. Through our discussion we have seen good reason to agree that both understanding is more valuable than knowledge, and that understanding only comes by way of thinking for yourself. Nevertheless, the understanding objection fails. The understanding objection fails because we are not required to do what is the best, only what is good enough. Often, what we can get through deference is good enough. We can get a true belief, a reasonable belief, and even knowledge, all by deferring. Knowing the answer to our question is a suitable place to stop our inquiry even if we could go farther and perhaps understand the answer as well. That said, these considerations do show why the stronger thesis, that it is wrong or inappropriate to think for yourself on matters where you lack expertise, is too strong. Here we see that there can be intellectual reasons to engage in first-person deliberation on matters where one lacks expertise. Doing so plays an important role in the cultivation of understanding. The value of understanding gives us reason to engage in deliberative inquiry even if it does not require that we do so. In the next chapter, we turn to our final objection and consider whether the cultivation of intellectual virtues shows that there is something wrong with our central conclusion.

In this chapter we examine the final objection to our central conclusion. According to this last objection, you must think for yourself, since failing to think for yourself means that you fail to develop your intellectual character. Having a good intellectual character is important, and we all have a duty to ourselves to cultivate our own intellectual character. However, according to this objection, the only way to do so is to think for yourself. Developing your intellectual character cannot happen by way of outsourcing your intellectual projects, it requires that you put in the work yourself. Since deference stands in the way of cultivating your intellectual virtue, there is a requirement to think for yourself.

The intellectual virtue objection is perhaps the most challenging objection to our central conclusion. We will examine several layers of response to it in this chapter. The first layer of response rejects the claim that our central conclusion stands in the way of cultivating our intellectual character. Here we need to remind ourselves that our central conclusion is compatible with still doing a great deal of thinking for yourself. Even though each of us has expertise in very limited domains, we still do a lot of thinking in those domains. In addition, many of our traditional intellectual virtues can actually be exercised and developed *through* deference. So, rather than deference

DOI: 10.4324/9781003369004-10

posing an obstacle to the development of these intellectual character traits, it can actually help to cultivate them. The second layer of response is more radical. It calls for a revisioning of our intellectual virtues in a way that captures the insights of social epistemology. This updated list of virtues highlights new and important traits to help individuals navigate the interdependent intellectual economy that we now inhabit.

MOTIVATING THE OBJECTION

Use it or lose it. That phrase is familiar enough. Growing up in Canada, I learned to speak French from a very early age. I even went to a French immersion school for a few years. Having taken some form of French up to and through high school, I was fairly fluent. After high school I didn't take any other French courses, and having moved to the US, my exposure to the French language went down exponentially. Now I find myself struggling to think of basic terms in French and I doubt that I would be able to put together too many well-formed sentences. What happened? I stopped reading in French, and I stopped speaking French. Those activities were critical to whatever skills and abilities I had with the language. I lost my fluency from a lack of use.

Something similar could be said of our minds more generally. We can think of our brains as a kind of muscle that requires training and development. If you stop using it, it atrophies and can no longer perform the needed tasks. Someone who defers to the experts about some matter doesn't think about it for themselves. They do not go through the process of acquiring and evaluating the relevant (direct) evidence on their own. The worry is that here too, if you stop doing those things, you will lose your ability to do them well. At the very least, you will fail to develop your mind to be all that it can be. Whatever your level of critical thinking ability, it will not improve without training, just as your ability to speak French won't improve without practice.

In "What is Enlightenment?" (1991/1784), Kant claimed that "enlightenment is man's emergence from his self-incurred immaturity. Immaturity is man's inability to make use of his understanding without the guidance of another." (54) One way to think about intellectual maturity is as having a cultivated intellectual character. Like learning to walk, or ride a bike, thinking might require the help of others to get started, but with maturity comes the ability to do it all on one's own – in this case, to be an independent thinker.[1] Continuing to outsource one's intellectual projects might look like continuing to use training wheels on your bike. It is supposed to be something that we outgrow as mature individuals, and the way to outgrow your intellectual immaturity is by cultivating your intellectual character.

A cultivated intellectual character is valuable, and it is something that is for everyone. According to King (2021), the importance of the intellectual virtues can be seen by the importance of thinking well. Good thinking affects one's relationships, citizenship, education, and success in life more generally. Since our actions are deeply connected to our beliefs, it is important for our beliefs to be good. One way to do so, is to have them be the product of a good intellectual character. Since relationships, citizenship, education, and success all matter to us, cultivating our intellectual character should matter to us all as well. We should all strive to develop excellent minds.

We first talked about intellectual virtues in Chapter 4 when we examined the autonomy objection. It's worth refreshing our minds regarding the nature of intellectual virtues.

There we followed Baehr's (2011) characterization of an intellectual virtue as "a character trait that contributes to its possessor's personal intellectual worth on account of its involving a positive psychological orientation toward epistemic goods." (102) Intellectual virtues help us in our intellectual pursuits. These character traits make us better off epistemically. Often, these intellectual traits were virtuous when they were a mean between extremes of both excess and deficiency, when the trait in question was had to an extent that was just right, what Aristotle called 'the golden mean.'

Virtues, both moral and intellectual, are developed. No one simply finds themselves virtuous. Cultivating virtue requires practice, habituation, and constant refinement. As we saw in Chapter 6, we can't simply acquire moral virtue through deferring on moral matters. Even if deference can give us the appropriate belief, it takes more than that to have the associated virtue. Character virtues have a more complicated cognitive profile. In addition to doing (or believing) the right thing, they require having the proper motivation and acting (or believing) for the right reasons, as well as being disposed to do so across a wide variety of circumstances.

So, developing intellectual virtue is something that takes work. In particular, cultivating your intellectual virtue seems to take a lot of thinking for yourself. Given all of this, it looks like someone who outsources a good deal of their intellectual projects is unlikely to be, or become, intellectually virtuous. Here too, use it or lose it may seem to apply.

Let's look at just one example to help motivate this point. Consider the intellectual virtue of perseverance. According to Heather Battaly (2017: 670), the trait of intellectual perseverance is "a disposition to overcome obstacles, so as to continue performing intellectual actions, in pursuit of one's intellectual goals."[2] When this trait is had to the appropriate extent (not too much or too little) and is motivated by a love of truth, it is an intellectual virtue. Essential to Battaly's account of intellectual perseverance is overcoming obstacles in inquiry. So, if one never encountered obstacles in inquiry, they would not be able to exercise and cultivate the virtue of intellectual perseverance. Agents with virtuous perseverance don't give up in their inquiry too soon, but they also don't stick with it too long either. Further, their efforts are guided by a love for the truth (rather than say their need to win an argument or impress others).

One way to not encounter obstacles in inquiry is to not think for yourself. If other people are engaging in inquiry on your behalf, then you aren't the one who is facing the obstacles! They are. So, individuals who defer will not cultivate their intellectual perseverance. They are not training their minds in the appropriate ways by not engaging in inquiry for themselves. So, it looks like not thinking for yourself thwarts the cultivation of intellectual perseverance. Further, these considerations may seem to hold for the other intellectual virtues as well. After all, how could one be open-minded, careful, or intellectually courageous without thinking for oneself? So, it looks like intellectual character development requires intellectual exercise, and the relevant exercise only comes by way of thinking for yourself.

This, then, is the intellectual virtue objection. In deferring to others, you stunt the development of your intellectual character. A virtuous intellectual character is quite valuable. So, in not thinking for yourself, you are depriving yourself of important epistemic goods. Because of this, people need to think for themselves. Those who don't, fail to do something important, and that is not OK.

Our response to the intellectual virtue objection will take place in several stages. The first line of response is to question the connection between our central conclusion and the cultivation of one's intellectual character. According to this response, our conclusion doesn't have the alleged consequences for one's intellectual character. The second line of response calls for a shift in how we think about intellectual virtues. According to this response, the objection considered here is mired in an overly individualistic conception of epistemology. Once we embrace a truly social epistemology, this will call for re-imagining what intellectual virtues look like. These socially enhanced intellectual virtues are fully compatible with our central conclusion. Taken together, we will see that we have strong reason to resist the intellectual virtue objection.

CULTIVATING INTELLECTUAL CHARACTER THROUGH DEFERENCE

Before looking at some candidates of intellectual virtues that you can exercise and cultivate without thinking for yourself, it is worth recollecting that the central conclusion argued for in this book does not imply that people should, or could, *never* think for themselves. Recall that the argument from expertise claimed that for almost any question you wanted to answer, someone else was better positioned to answer that question. However, for some questions, you *are* in as good of an epistemic position as anyone is to answer them. There we pointed to questions about your personal life and your immediate environment in particular. While these domains make up a small proportion of the kinds of questions you might consider, you likely often consider questions in these domains. So, our central conclusion is consistent with you still doing quite a bit of thinking for yourself, it is just that the kinds of questions that you should think about for yourself are quite limited in scope. Nevertheless, it is compatible with our central conclusion that you are still required to do a significant amount of thinking for yourself.

For instance, recall our analogy with Rico the homeowner. While there may be very few tasks that Rico takes on himself (taking out the trash, changing easy-to-reach lightbulbs, etc.), he may quite frequently confront those tasks. So, even if all of the intellectual virtues require thinking for yourself, our central conclusion does not automatically preclude the development of your intellectual character. It is compatible with our conclusion that a good deal of thinking for yourself is still called for (even if there are not many domains that call for it). That is, the limited domains where thinking for yourself is called for still provide sufficient opportunity to develop your intellectual character.

So, our central conclusion is consistent with your mind still getting a lot of exercise, enough to cultivate your intellectual character. On top of that, it seems plausible that some intellectual virtues can be embodied without doing too much thinking for yourself. That is, some intellectual virtues seem compatible with, and are even exercised through, deference to others. In Chapter 4, we saw reason to think that developing the intellectual virtue of epistemic autonomy was compatible with significant deference. To recap what was argued there, the virtue of epistemic autonomy consists of making good judgments in inquiry (when to think for yourself, and when to rely on others), to conduct your inquiry in line with those judgments, and to do so out of a love for the truth. One's situation in life can be such that deference is often the way to go (recall once more the argument from expertise). In such cases, decisions to defer can be motivated by one's love of the truth and desire to get the answer right. So, such deference amounts to exercising the intellectual virtue of epistemic autonomy – it is an instance of good executive management of one's inquiry, all done with the proper motivation.

Intellectual humility is another intellectual virtue whose development seems compatible with deferring to others. According to Whitcomb et al. (2017), intellectual humility consists of being appropriately attentive to, and owning, one's intellectual limitations.[3] On this view, humble thinkers acknowledge their limitations, care about them, and take them seriously. Such intellectual humility can be exercised in deferring to others who are better placed epistemically to determine the answer to the question at hand. Often, the humble thing to do is to acknowledge that you are not as well positioned to answer your question as someone else is. In acknowledging this and turning to the expertise of others, you are owning your own intellectual limitations, whether that be limitations in evidence or limitations in your ability to evaluate that evidence. The result of owning these limitations is deference to someone who isn't so limited. So, intellectual humility can also be exercised through deference to others.[4]

Another intellectual virtue that fits well with our central conclusion is curiosity. Following King (2021) we can see the virtue of curiosity as having a healthy appetite for knowledge.[5] Curious individuals have questions, and they want to know the answers. They are not indifferent, nor are they intellectually gluttonous. As we have seen, there are different ways that one might pursue an answer to their question. They might think about it for themselves, or they might defer to someone else. With the interest of gaining knowledge, deference is often the way to go. Deference is often much more likely to deliver knowledge than one's own individual inquiry, and it also allows one to get the answers to many more questions than one would ever be able to answer for themselves. So, deferring on many matters seems precisely like what a curious person would do; deferring is a good route to satisfying one's curiosity.[6]

Open-mindedness is yet another intellectual virtue that can be exercised and developed in and through deference. Following Baehr (2011: 152) we can understand open-mindedness as being willing and able to transcend your own perspective and to take seriously the perspectives of others.[7] So, open-minded people are willing and able to take on other perspectives – to listen to them, to seek to understand them, and to allow them to challenge and shape their own views. Open-minded individuals listen to and learn from others. Since open-mindedness consists of an eagerness to have one's perspective enriched by others, it is another intellectual virtue that can be exercised through deference. One can be open-minded in both who one listens to as well as how they listen to them.

While not exhaustive, this brief survey shows that many central intellectual virtues *can* actually be exhibited through deference. Rather than impeding the development of one's intellectual character, deferring to others can often be the way to cultivate it. What this shows is that following our central conclusion will not prevent one from developing, or maintaining, many central intellectual character virtues. When we couple this insight with the idea that our central conclusion is still compatible with doing a great deal of thinking for yourself, we have good reason to believe that following the central conclusion of the book will not stunt the development of one's intellectual character.

CARTESIAN EPISTEMOLOGY AND SOCIAL EPISTEMOLOGY

Let's turn to our second line of response. According to this line of response to the intellectual virtue objection, we need to re-think what the intellectual virtues look like. The role of the intellectual virtues is to help us acquire, maintain, and distribute intellectual goods like true beliefs and knowledge. Intellectual virtues make us, and those around us, better off epistemically. In particular, many of the traditional intellectual virtues are focused on helping us come to find the answers to our questions – on helping us inquire well. The intellectual virtues help us to reliably get to true beliefs while avoiding false ones in our own individual inquiry.

However, given what we have seen about the cognitive division of labor, not everyone needs to be involved on the front lines of these intellectual endeavors. As social creatures we do our best when we work together, and the same is true of us intellectually. Given this, we needn't all be on the front lines of inquiry as the traditional list of intellectual virtues presupposes. For instance, many of the traditional intellectual virtues exist as virtues because they are being viewed from an overly individualistic epistemic paradigm. What is being assumed is that we are each involved in carrying out the relevant inquiry for ourselves. Such a paradigm ignores the fact that we are social knowers, and it ignores the many ways in which we have divided up our intellectual labors. While there are qualities that we want our knowledge producers to have, not everyone is, or needs to be, a knowledge producer. For instance, some might be involved in intellectual endeavors, but be focused on knowledge distribution instead of knowledge production (e.g. science communicators). Others might have their role primarily as knowledge consumers. The intellectual traits that we want knowledge producers to have (or at least those traits that we are most concerned with them having) can differ from those we desire of knowledge distributors and knowledge consumers. Given the division of labor in the cognitive economy, what intellectual character traits we should strive for will differ depending on our role. So, the intellectual division of labor should lead us to revisit our list of intellectual virtues. The traditional list is a kind of one-size-fits-all set of character traits. A better list is more tailored to our individual intellectual roles. Indeed, many virtue epistemologists have shifted to examining more social intellectual virtues.[8] In doing so, we may find that the character traits it is most important that we have differ from those on the traditional list, and that they differ based upon one's intellectual role. We can think of this shift like the shift from an individual sport to a team sport.[9] While both types of sports involve athletes, the characteristics that make one a good team player differ from those that make one a good individual player. And depending on your role on the team, still more different characteristics may be relevant for your success and the success of the team.

So, what might intellectual virtues look like within a more socially enhanced picture of epistemology? In the next section, we will explore several proposed intellectual virtues that appreciate the deep intellectual interdependence that we have.

SOCIAL INTELLECTUAL VIRTUES

When I was in elementary school, I remember students asking our math teacher why we had to learn multiplication, division, and other mathematical calculations since we could simply use a calculator instead. The response was always something like, "well, you are not going to carry around a calculator with you everywhere you go." Fast forward more years than I would like to admit, and almost everyone is carrying around a calculator everywhere they go. In fact, the calculator function is but a small fraction of the things that your phone can do. Times change, and with changing times comes a change with respect to the needed skills. For instance, now many who were great at doing long division by hand, need help updating their phone, downloading a new app, and so forth.

Other societal shifts are relevant here as well. As individuals began to specialize, and hyper-specialize, the best way to achieve our intellectual goals has also shifted. Before turning to the intellectual case, think first about our day-to-day living. At one time, it was important to be able to hunt, farm, make clothing, and so forth all for yourself. Living a good life in that environment required it. But things have changed. The way that we get our food and clothing is drastically different. We've outsourced those projects. In this environment, different skills are relevant. Now it is more important to be a good shopper – to navigate all the food and clothing options that present themselves to you well. The same holds for inquiry. While there was perhaps a time when we had to rely heavily on ourselves in inquiry, that's not the information environment that we occupy. Now we 'shop' for information. This shift in how we acquire answers to our questions comes with a shift in what skills are the most relevant to our success. Just as we have shifted from being food and shelter producers to primarily being food and shelter consumers, so too have we shifted from being knowledge producers to being primarily knowledge consumers.

The traditional intellectual virtues are perhaps seen as best suited for individuals who are themselves engaged in inquiry – individuals who are in the business of knowledge discovery – the knowledge producers. But, as we have seen, not everyone is, or needs to be, on the front lines of inquiry. Further, even those who are on the front lines in some domains will not be so situated regarding other questions in other domains. Even those with expertise only have expertise in a narrow range of issues. We have seen the importance of a cognitive division of labor. Our epistemic interdependence comes with a need to rethink what intellectual virtues look like today, where we appreciate that our intellectual flourishing is a social matter.[10] Green (2016) notes this shift, claiming the following: "If one expects to depend on others and embraces opportunities to think in interdependent ways, to demonstrate one's initiative and judiciousness from a socially embedded position, then agency will take a very different form than it would otherwise." (222)

So, social epistemology calls for a reimagined list of intellectual virtues. As we have seen, the informational economy contains an intellectual division of labor. Different people investigate different questions with the result of more knowledge for everyone. In this informational economy there are producers, distributors, and consumers of information. There are those who we rely on to answer our questions, those that translate those answers, and those of us who listen to the answers. Our re-envisioned list of intellectual virtues needs to look at what character traits we would want people in these different roles to have – character traits that would facilitate the epistemic flourishing of the whole community.

Let's first think about knowledge producers and distributors, those who we depend on for getting us the answers to our questions, before turning to knowledge consumers. Jason Kawall (2002) has criticized virtue theorists for neglecting to give adequate attention to what he calls "other-regarding" virtues, virtues such as honesty, sincerity, integrity, and creativity. These other-regarding virtues are focused on bringing about intellectual goods for, or in, other people. Kawall draws the parallel with other-regarding moral virtues like benevolence, compassion, and justice, which aim primarily at bringing about the flourishing of others. (258)

Similarly, Croce (2017) discusses a range of intellectual virtues for experts (or epistemic authorities) such as sensitivity to the epistemic inferior subject's needs and resources, intellectual generosity, and maieutic ability. According to Croce, experts have virtues attuned to finding and facing new problems in their domain of expertise, but there are also virtues to have which are directed toward novices. These novice-oriented virtues assist those who are depending on the experts for their expertise and facilitate the transfer of epistemic goods.[11]

Along these same lines, Byerly (2021) explores the virtues that make experts intellectually dependable. As he notes, "it is one thing to possess relevant evidence or arguments and another to share these effectively with those who depend on one to do so". (24) Byerly identifies five traits as good candidates for intellectual virtues of intellectual dependability: intellectual benevolence, intellectual transparency, communitive clarity, sensitivity to one's audience, and epistemic guidance. Each of these five traits is primarily aimed at bringing about epistemic goods in someone else. Intellectual benevolence is a stable and refined motivation to bring about intellectual goods in others. Intellectual transparency is a tendency to share one's own perspective with others so that their own inquiry is enhanced. Communicative clarity aims to avoid confusion in communication so as to better transfer epistemic goods (i.e. true beliefs, knowledge, etc.). Along these same lines, sensitivity to one's audience is manifested by carefully adjusting one's testimony to best deliver those intellectual goods. This amounts to paying attention to the intellectual abilities and background knowledge of one's audience, and accommodating them in communication. Finally, epistemic guidance involves helping shape the inquiry of others so that it is more likely to be successful. (35–6)

This quick survey serves to illustrate that there are traits that it is beneficial for knowledge producers and distributors to have. Just as there are traits which facilitate the production and distribution of knowledge and other intellectual goods, there are also traits which facilitate their reception. We also need to think about information consumers and what traits they ought to have. After all, this is where most of us find ourselves, at least most of the time. Just as the experts should have the virtues of intellectual dependability, laypeople ought to have virtues of intellectual receptivity.

We have already seen how some traditional intellectual virtues have important social elements. Epistemic autonomy, intellectual humility, curiosity, and open-mindedness all have important roles to play in facilitating the acquisition of intellectual goods from others. However, it is also worth briefly highlighting a few other plausible candidates for socially oriented intellectual virtues that facilitate the reception of knowledge. These character traits help individuals be good consumers in the marketplace of ideas.

Let's start with a virtue that we might call intellectual discernment. Those who have the virtue of intellectual discernment trust others well. They are neither too skeptical nor are they too gullible in listening to others. They are aware of who can be trusted on any given matter, as well as what kind of intellectual goods they will be able to deliver (true belief, knowledge, etc.).[12] Robertson (2016) calls a similar trait 'testimonial virtue.' She writes:

> The aim of testimonial virtue is to trust those who are trustworthy (i.e., competent and honest or sincere) and distrust those who are untrustworthy (i.e., incompetent or lying). Put another way, the goal is to grant epistemic authority only to those deserving of it.
>
> (130)

Having this virtue enables one to navigate the seas of information well. Further, it is something that requires training. Robertson continues:

> persons who possess testimonial virtue have a cultivated disposition to exercise due caution in receiving testimony and a trained (but reflectively revisable) sensibility for whom is to be trusted in what circumstances backed by relevant knowledge for making that judgment.
>
> (130)

A related social virtue concerns how you interpret others. According to King (2021), intellectual charity is the character virtue concerning treating others as you would want to be treated in your intellectual activities. While the application of intellectual charity goes beyond how we listen to and interpret others, there are ramifications here as well. For instance, King argues that charitable individuals will work hard to interpret the views of others in the best possible light (particularly when there is disagreement), attribute as much intelligence and intellectual virtue as we reasonably can to our interlocutors, and to not be too quick to attribute the errors of others to defects in their intelligence or intellectual character. Charitable thinkers do not 'straw-man'[13] the arguments of others, but follow the principle of charity. According to the principle of charity, we should interpret the ideas and arguments of others in the most plausible way possible, giving their thoughts the best and most credible interpretation. Being a charitable thinker clearly connects with other intellectual virtues like open-mindedness. Being charitable also has clear intellectual benefits. It helps one to avoid the errors of confirmation bias and belief bias. Charitably taking on information from different perspectives facilitates finding the truth.

'If you're not mad, you're not paying attention.' This phrase highlights the importance of being properly attuned to the world around you. According to Gardiner (2022), "Proper attunement is paying attention to the right things in the right way, at the right time; being sensitive to significant features and ignoring what should be ignored." (49)

It is easy to be overwhelmed by all of the information we have at our fingertips. It is important to be attuned to what is important. As Gardiner notes, our habits of attention are malleable – they can become better or worse, and these changes can be deliberate or unintentional. Our attention can be shaped by society and by ourselves through education, practice, and habituation.

We can also assess attention along various dimensions. First, we can think about the attention given to any one speaker or source of information. Those with the virtue of attention pay careful attention for cues regarding sincerity (or insincerity) or competence (or incompetence). Second, we can think about the sources of information that one pays attention to. The attentive person is not just zeroed in on one source of information, they pay attention to different perspectives. Further, they pay attention to a wide variety of issues. For instance, attentive people are not simply focused on the outcomes of sporting events. Attentive people are plugged into informational networks that provide extensive coverage reliability.[14]

In her book *Epistemic Injustice* (2007), Miranda Fricker identified and illustrated a harmful epistemic vice. According to Fricker, epistemic injustice occurs when one is harmed in their capacity as a knower. While the wrong here can be more than merely intellectual, the intellectual harm is the focus. For instance, testimonial injustice is one species of epistemic injustice that occurs when one is given a lower (or higher[15]) degree of credibility than one deserves due to prejudice. So, for instance, when a sexist colleague gives the testimony of their female co-workers less weight, they exhibit epistemic injustice and treat their female co-workers unfairly by not giving them the intellectual credibility that they deserve. This is an intellectual wrong since it is not giving their word the appropriate evidential weight.

Against this backdrop, Fricker proposes the virtue of testimonial justice. Individuals who possess the virtue of testimonial justice are disposed to critically reflect on the ways in which prejudice may be influencing how credible they view a given testifier and make the needed adjustments. Such reflection can bring to light cognitive dissonance between one's beliefs related to the credibility of the speaker and spontaneously formed judgments about their credibility.[16] In properly distributing credibility, hearers are less likely to be misled and more likely to gain insights from others.[17]

Different roles in the information economy highlight different characteristics that it is valuable for individuals to have. The flourishing of our intellectual community occurs when individuals have the intellectual virtues that are suited to their

Why It's OK Not to Think for Yourself

role in the intellectual division of labor. What we have seen here is that what the ideal knowledge producer and distributor looks like is different from what the ideal knowledge consumer looks like. This calls for a shift in our goals in terms of our desired intellectual character. In this intellectually interdependent world, most of us are primarily knowledge consumers. This fact calls for a shift in the kinds of intellectual character traits that we should strive for and those that are most relevant to our lives. We need to think beyond the traditional list of intellectual virtues whose focus is primarily on knowledge production.[18]

THE UPSHOT

In this chapter we have examined the intellectual virtue objection to our central conclusion. According to this objection, thinking for yourself is essential for developing your intellectual character. Since it is important and valuable to have a cultivated intellectual character, we need to think for ourselves. Our response came in several layers. First, we noted that our central conclusion is still consistent with individuals doing a great deal of thinking for themselves. Even if there are not many domains where one should think for themselves, one nevertheless does a lot of thinking in those limited domains where one does have expertise. So, even if thinking for yourself is required for developing one's intellectual virtue, there isn't a conflict here. Second, we saw that many of the core intellectual virtues can be exercised through deference. Intellectual humility, epistemic autonomy, curiosity, and open-mindedness all appear to be cultivated through deferring to others who are in a better epistemic position to answer the question at hand. Our second layer of response argued that an appreciation of our social nature requires us to rethink which intellectual virtues are most relevant today. The traditional list of intellectual virtues was focused on individuals conducting their own inquiry and producing knowledge. Given a rich informational environment where we typically rely on others in inquiry calls for an enriched set of characteristics to help individuals flourish in this environment. Here we highlighted several intellectual virtues that are socially focused and pay attention to our role in the informational economy. While we should resist the intellectual virtue objection, it too shows us why the stronger thesis, that it is wrong or inappropriate to think for yourself about matters where you lack expertise, is overly strong. Deliberative inquiry as a layperson can help one to cultivate their intellectual character. While these reasons to think for ourselves don't have it that we are required to do so, they do indicate why it can nevertheless be valuable to do so.

That's the book. Let's quickly retrace the journey and draw out several take-aways.

We began by distinguishing two different ways that one can conduct inquiry: they can think for themselves, or they can defer. An individual thinks for themselves when they gather and appreciate the relevant direct reasons. They defer when they believe on the basis of someone else's say-so, without hearing the reasons why that individual believes what they do. With this distinction in hand, we saw two arguments for the conclusion that it is OK not to think for yourself — that thinking for yourself is overrated. The argument from expertise claimed that for almost any question you want to answer, there is someone who is better positioned to answer that question. So, given your goal of getting the answer, it is perfectly fine to take the more reliable route to the answer and defer to the experts. The argument from evidential swamping made the case that what we should believe about a topic is based on what the experts believe; that thinking for yourself won't change what it is rational for you to believe. If thinking for yourself doesn't change what you should believe, then it is OK not to do it. The bulk of the book then laid out and responded to a series of objections to this admittedly counter-intuitive conclusion. If I'm right, then the objections all fail,

DOI: 10.4324/9781003369004-11

and our central conclusion stands. What should we make of that fact? Well, here are a couple take-aways.

1 Deference to the experts shouldn't be seen as lazy or inadequate

It can be tempting to value someone who 'does their own research' over someone who merely defers to the experts. Given what has been argued here, however, that is a mistake. Deference is typically the more reliable route to the answer. While deference can be done out of laziness, we have also seen that it can be motivated by a love of truth, and that it can exhibit a number of intellectual virtues like open-mindedness, intellectual humility, curiosity, and even epistemic autonomy. Deference deserves a better reputation. It is often the responsible way to conduct inquiry, just like outsourcing your home repair projects is often the responsible choice.

2 Thinking for yourself is still important

While the focus of the book has been defending *not* thinking for yourself, throughout the book we have seen reasons why it is also valuable to do so. Our central conclusion should not be interpreted as being *against* thinking for yourself. After all, it is only by thinking for yourself that you can come to gain understanding, and understanding is intellectually valuable. Further, at least some intellectual virtues seem to be developed only through thinking for yourself. So, while thinking for yourself is overrated, it is not to be abandoned altogether. It still has a role in our intellectual lives.

For instance, throughout the book you have been invited to think for yourself about a number of interesting issues in epistemology. I think you will be better off for having done so, even if the book is (perhaps somewhat ironically) about not thinking for yourself.

Notes

INTRODUCTION

1. https://jmp.princeton.edu/news/2017/some-thoughts-and-advice-our-students-and-all-students#:-:text=think%20for%20yourself (accessed 05/29/2023).

2. See Brighouse (2005), Ebels-Duggan (2014), Elgin (2013), Nussbaum (2017), Pritchard (2022), Ryan (2021), and Seigel (1988).

3. Huemer (2005) notes the following quotes from leading introduction to philosophy texts (among others):

   "In this conversation, all sides of an issue should receive a fair hearing, and then you, the reader, should make up your own minds on the issue."

   (Pojman 1991: 5)

   "My hope is that exposure to this argumentative give-and-take will encourage students to take part in the process themselves, and through this practice to develop their powers of philosophical reasoning."

   (Feinberg 1996: xi)

4. We will return to the issue of knowledge and its relation in inquiry in Chapter 8.

5. The distinction here parallels the distinction between first-order evidence and higher-order evidence. See Christensen (2010), Kelly (2010), and Matheson (2009).

6. Epistemologist Richard Feldman is known for coining the motto "evidence of evidence is evidence." This is, of course, not without contention. Some philosophers in the epistemology of testimony see testimony more like a direct kind of reason. Here, the debate is between reductionists and non-reductionists about testimony. Non-reductionists

see testimony more like perception or memory, whereas reductionists place more demands on testimonial sources than these other sources. On the non-reductionist picture, testimony can be seen as giving both a direct and indirect reason. Even here, though, the direct reasons given by testimony still seem importantly different than other types of direct reasons. For this reason, we will simply treat them as indirect reasons in this book. What is more important for our purposes is dividing the relevant types of reasons as we have, rather than the particular labels that we give each type of reason.

7. Chapter 1 will look in much more detail at the rationality of believing on the basis of indirect reasons alone. For more on this picture of testimony as a placeholder for one's reasons, see Matheson (forthcoming) and Rowley (2018).

8. We will spend much more time on this point in Chapter 8.

9. See Anderson (1995) and Kitcher (2001).

10. This is what Goldman (2001) considered cognitive expertise, as opposed to performative expertise. For an excellent survey of the literature on expertise, see Watson (2021).

11. See Frances and Matheson (2019).

12. While expertise comes in degrees, and so no one is simply a flat-out expert or a flat-out novice, for ease of expression, we will often ignore this fact and simply talk about experts and novices without such qualifications.

13. See Fricker (2006b), Goldman (2016), and Hardwig (1985).

14. The way that I am using the term 'expert' here has a great deal in common with how many in the literature use the term 'epistemic authority'. The term 'epistemic authority' comes from Zagzebski (2012). For a helpful discussion of the differences between experts and epistemic authorities, see Croce (2017).

15. In addition, you might have trained expertise in some other domain.

16. See Dellsén (2020, 2021) for an extensive argument for why experts should think for themselves.

1

1. At least by his own lights he was able to. While most agree with Descartes' proof of his existence, most are skeptical of the way that he proceeds from there.

2. Goldman calls this 'individual doxastic agent social epistemology.'

3. Goldman calls this 'collective doxastic agent social epistemology.'
4. For a discussion of how an individualistic epistemology like evidentialism can fit within this more social epistemological picture, see Matheson (forthcoming).
5. For an extensive defense, see Goldberg (2010).
6. For an overview of the epistemology of testimony, see Lackey (2006).
7. This follows Zagzebski's (2012) justification thesis which puts this point in terms of conscientiousness.
8. This is Grasswick's (2020) example.
9. This is also Grasswick's (2020) example.
10. This term comes from Dogramaci (2012) who credits Karl Schafer.
11. See Hardwig (1985: 338).
12. More carefully put, it is still about our reasons, but it is our reasons about the experts' reasons that are doing the epistemological work.
13. This argument comes from Matheson (2021b), though the example is borrowed from Kelly (2011).
14. This too comes from Matheson (2021b).
15. One way that this type of reasoning has been used in philosophy is the common consent argument for God's existence. For discussion, see Kelly (2011), Matheson (2021b), and Zagzebski (2011).
16. For more on the Condorcet Jury Theorem and this example, see Estlund (1994). See also Hazlett (2016).
17. Surowiecki (2004: 4).
18. See Surowiecki (2004), Sunstein (2008), Elster and Landemore (2012), and Solomon (2010) for many more examples and discussion.
19. www.imdb.com/chart/top/ (accessed 05/29/2023).
20. For a discussion of the ways in which social pressure can affect beliefs in a community, see Joshi (2021).

2

1. A similar argument is given regarding critical thinking by Huemer (2005).
2. This case comes from Matheson (2022).
3. For example, see Constantin and Grundmann (2018), Grundmann (2021), and Zagzebski (2012).
4. Beyond getting the answer wrong, some additional dangers in thinking for yourself include self-licensing (DiPaolo forthcoming-a), epistemic injustice (Matheson 2022), and falling prey to conspiracy theories (DiPaolo forthcoming-a, Grundmann 2021, Levy 2022a).

5. Note that this would not only involve all of Gretzky's games, but also all of the games where other players played as well.

6. This case appears in Matheson (2022).

7. This case appears in Matheson (2022).

8. For instance, see Pillay (2010).

9. For instance, see Goldman (2001), Anderson (2011), Grundmann (forthcoming), and Martini (2020).

10. See Shanteau (1992), Martini (2020), and Goldman (2001).

11. This is what Nguyen (2018b) calls a 'litmus test' for expertise.

12. We will return to this issue when we consider the Socratic objection in Chapter 6.

13. See Kitcher (1993) in addition to Nguyen (2020) for more on indirect calibration.

14. See also Goldman (2001), Martini (2020), and Shanteau (2000).

15. See also Anderson (2011: 149) and Oreskes (2019: 128–9).

16. See Ballantyne (2022) for an explanation of some of the worries here.

3

1. Strictly speaking, what you should believe about a matter is entirely determined by what your evidence about the state of expert opinion is. So, you are reasonable in believing according to what your evidence supports about the state of the debate. That said, for ease of prose I will typically just talk about the state of the debate.

2. See Cook et al. (2016).

3. This follows Matheson, McElreath, and Nobis (2018).

4. You might worry about whether there even are experts in these domains. We will turn to that issue in Chapter 6.

5. This is the central lesson from the literature on the epistemology of disagreement. For an overview, see Matheson (2015) and Frances and Matheson (2019).

6. Remember, I never said I was against thinking for yourself. I'm just arguing that you don't need to do so.

7. See also Goldberg (2022) for another argument about the impact of experts on the rationality of novice beliefs.

8. It may sound at this point that there is no reason to think for yourself. That's not correct. We will see reasons why it is valuable to think

for yourself in Chapters 8 and 9. However, while there are reasons to think for yourself, they do not show that thinking for yourself is necessary. It is still OK not to.

9. See the Introduction as well as Dellsén (2020, 2021).

4

1. For an excellent overview, see Christman (2020).
2. For a thorough overview, see Hinchman (1996).
3. Epistemic autonomy has more recently began to receive much more attention in the philosophical literature. See Zagzebski (2012) and Matheson and Lougheed (2021a). For an overview of the philosophical issues related to epistemic autonomy, see Matheson and Lougheed (2021b).
4. In addition to the authors that follow, see Ahlstrom-Vij (2013: 92), Code (1991), and McMyler (2011).
5. Millgram falls into this camp as well. He claims, "because we are now in the business of deploying cooperatively assembled arguments, where no one is competent to assess the argument as a whole, older ideals of autonomy, intellectual or otherwise, no long have much to do with today's realities." (2015: 15).
6. See Nedelsky (1989), Encabo (2008), Elzinga (2019), and Grasswick (2018) for the compatibility of autonomy and relying on others. Zagzebski (2012) also argues that epistemic autonomy is actually incompatible with self-reliance.
7. If you want to check it out, see Aad et al. (2015).
8. Here, I follow Grasswick (2018) and the distinction between developmental and constitutive relational autonomy.
9. See Westlund (2012), Elgin (2013, 2021), and Grasswick (2018).
10. For more on relational autonomy, see Grasswick (2018) and Mackenzie and Stoljar (2000).
11. See Elgin (2013), Encabo (2008), and Grasswick (2018) for more on this point.
12. Code (2006).
13. See Elgin (2015) for an argument that our epistemic success is significantly dependent upon our intellectual community.
14. In addition, we can think of the history of the educational system in the US, which has been littered with obstacles for both women and

minority students. These obstacles make achieving their intellectual goals more difficult than they need be.

15. A further way in which this sense of epistemic autonomy is under threat concerns epistemic injustice. Epistemic injustice occurs when an individual is wronged in their capacity as a knower. See Fricker (2007) and Medina (2012). What goes wrong in a case of epistemic injustice is, as Grasswick puts it, an "inappropriate denial or degradation of another's epistemic autonomy." (Grasswick 2018: 197).

16. The ultimate goal of restricting such evidence is justice – so that people get fair treatment. However, the best route to having just verdicts is by way of having jurors with true beliefs. So while the ultimate goal of withholding such evidence isn't the mental states of the jurors, their beliefs do play an important role.

17. Additionally, sometimes you are given information that you didn't ask for. In these cases, too, the idea is that your inquiry has been interfered with, without your consent, but to help you meet your goals of attaining true beliefs and avoiding false ones. For instance, you might be required to sit through a certain presentation and receive information that you did not have any interest in hearing.

18. Alvin Goldman, a leading figure in social epistemology, maintains that these social features of our epistemological projects make epistemic paternalism necessary, and at least sometimes desirable. (1991: 127) For an extended defense, see Ahlstrom-Vij (2013). See also Joly Chock and Matheson (2020) for a clear case of permissible epistemic paternalism.

19. See also Brinkman (2022).

20. Virtue epistemologists distinguish between faculty virtues and character virtues. Here, I am understanding intellectual virtues as character virtues.

21. For a fuller treatment of intellectual virtues, see Code (1987), Zagzebski (1996), Roberts and Wood (2010), Baehr (2011), and King (2021).

22. We will return to discussing intellectual virtues, and doing so in more detail, in Chapter 9 where we examine the objection from intellectual virtues. There we will consider a host of intellectual virtues, and one's intellectual character more generally. The concern here is just with the virtue of epistemic autonomy.

23. See Ebels-Duggan (2014), Grasswick (2018), King (2021), Matheson and Lougheed (2021a), Roberts and Wood (2010), and Zagzebski

(2012, 2013). For a critical discussion of alternative accounts of epistemic autonomy as an intellectual virtue, see Matheson (2021c).

24. This follows Matheson (2021c).

25. In addition, Roberts and Wood (2010) claim that an epistemically autonomous individual is "properly regulated by others" (260) and that epistemic autonomy "involves a reasonable, active use of guidance from another." (267) On their account too, epistemic autonomy is an intellectual virtue that reflects the social nature of our intellectual practices. (257) So, to be epistemically autonomous is to be both an integrated and independent thinker.

26. While Battaly (2021) divorces the virtues of epistemic autonomy and intellectual independence, she still sees them as compatible. Battaly sees these two twin intellectual traits as being intimately related, not in competition with each other.

27. For instance, King (2021) does claim that it would be deficient if one failed to independently think about matters of morality, parenting, and philosophy. (99) We will set this issue aside for now, but will return to consider this in Chapter 7 as part of the Socratic objection.

5

1. See Joshi (2021: 38).

2. Joshi's primary concern with free-riding is with individuals who disagree with an accepted view of some matter, but don't register their dissent due to social pressure. but the same concern applies to those who simply don't put in the intellectual effort of their own. Joshi's concern is with individuals who fail to reveal their evidence to the community, but our concern runs even deeper – with individuals who fail to even gather evidence of their own in the first place.

3. See Hazlett (2016) for an argument along these lines.

4. See Ranalli (2019) for discussion, though not an endorsement, of the idea. See List and Pettit (2004) for discussion of a distinct problem regarding intellectual free-riding and the Condorcet Jury Theorem. The puzzle that List and Pettit are concerned with is that the jury theorem gives individuals reason to believe on the basis of what others believe. However, insofar as individuals take those reasons, they then cease to reason independently, and the reasons to believe others (afforded by the jury theorem) thereby go away.

5. This is a point also made by Ranalli (2020: 158).
6. For more on this point see Millgram (2015: ch. 2). Milgram argues that the Enlightenment has been its own undoing. In getting people to think for themselves we have created specialists, and hyperspecialists, which now render us unable to think for ourselves about a great deal.
7. See Ballantyne (2018, 2019), DiPaolo (2022), and Gerken (2018).
8. See Ballantyne (2019: 370) and DiPaolo (2022: 226).
9. DiPaolo (2022: 238).
10. See Hannon (2022) for more on this point.
11. For more, see Dunning (2011).
12. Dunning (2022: 210).
13. For more on this point, see Ahlstrom-Vij (2019), Brennan (2014), de Ridder (2021), and Goodin and List (2001).
14. For now, you'll have to just take my word on the matter. We will return to this issue, and discuss it in detail in Chapter 8.

6

1. This example comes from Howell (2014).
2. See Driver (2006), Crisp (2014), Hills (2009), Hopkins (2007), and McGrath (2009). For an overview of the debate, see Hills (2013).
3. See Hopkins (2011) and Sibley (1965). For an overview of the debate, see Robson (2013).
4. See Hazlett (2016) and van Wietmarschen (2018).
5. See Callahan (2022).
6. See Ranalli (2019).
7. See also Hazlett (2017). Similarly, Joseph Shieber (2010) argues that Kant's dictum to "think for yourself" should be limited to philosophical, moral, and mathematical matters.
8. See McGrath (2009), Enoch (2014: 232) and Mogensen (2017: 263).
9. At least not in a straightforward way. One might make the case that each still connects to normative issues.
10. For more on this point, see Matheson, McElreath, and Nobis (2018).
11. Brinkman (2022) also makes this point, though his primary concern is with political deference.
12. This is an example that often gets used for a case of pure moral deference.
13. See McGrath (2009) and Smith (2000).

14. Considering the case of mathematics also shows that this explanation fails to distinguish the relevant cases. It fails to draw the line between cases of appropriate and inappropriate deference where the objector believes it should be drawn.

15. For a rejection of the idea that relativism supports a pessimistic view of aesthetic testimony, see Meskin (2004: 80–4) and Laetz (2008: 360–1).

16. See Shafer-Landau (1998) for a nice statement of the case against ethical subjectivism. See McGrath (2009) for its application to the issue of moral testimony.

17. Relatedly, some have taken the problem to indicate a kind of non-cognitivism about morality – that moral claims are not true or false. Here I am only dealing with realist diagnoses of the issue.

18. For more on the potential unreliability of experts, see Koppl (2018) and Watson (2021).

19. For further discussion on the existence of philosophical expertise, see Goldman (2001), Coady (2002), and Fumerton (2010).

20. As Howell (2014) points out, however, deference in these cases seems to be more problematic, rather than less problematic. We would find it quite troubling if someone believed that torturing innocent children to pass the time is wrong, only on the basis of someone else's say so. This particular example might be a case of a self-evident moral truth that is easily available.

21. A related worry is that deference in these Socratic domains makes us too vulnerable with respect to these important issues. This vulnerability objection will be the focus of the next chapter.

22. See Howell (2014).

23. We will examine a parallel objection concerning your intellectual virtue in Chapter 9.

24. Howell (2014) makes this point as well. Also see Robson (2012) for a discussion.

25. For similar reasons, political deference might be seen to preclude one from being a good democratic citizen. See Hazlett (2016) for one such argument. For defenses of the legitimacy of such political deference, see Brinkman (2022) and Fuerstein (2013).

26. To help see this, we can think about cases concerning discrimination or harassment. Often it is much easier for someone other than the

potential perpetrator to evaluate whether discrimination or harassment has occurred. In such cases, deference to a neutral party seems like a wise course of action. We are likely not to detect our own discrimination. For instance, determining whether a given joke was racist or sexist is probably best done by someone other than the joke teller.

27. In fact, the explanation that moral deference is problematic because it precludes moral understanding is one of the more predominant views in the literature on moral testimony. The discussion in Chapter 8 could easily belong here instead, though we will go into much greater detail by giving it a chapter of its own.

7

1. Although, even if I drive myself, I am still vulnerable. In driving myself I am relying on my car, on the roads to be functional, on other drivers to behave themselves, and so forth.

2. See Millgram (2015).

3. Levy (2022b) examines two recent cases in the academic context: a hoax journal submission and fabricated social media testimony. Lackey (2021b) examines the problem of predatory experts. More on this later.

4. This example comes from McBrayer (2022).

5. This example comes from DiPaolo (2022: 236).

6. Further still, as several philosophers have noted, those who are marginalized in society have an even greater vulnerability here. See Grasswick (2020), Lackey (2018), Medina (2012), and Fricker (2007).

7. For an argument that we cannot be certain of our own mental states, see Williamson's (2000) anti-luminosity argument.

8. Of course, the skeptic does not agree. Central to many versions of skepticism is the idea that fallible reasons are insufficient to make our beliefs rational. There is a lot to be said about the arguments for and against skepticism, but not here.

9. See Hardwig (1985: 338–40).

10. Recall our example of baking the complicated dessert when the lifeline of Martha Stewart is available. You are better off trusting Martha to complete the dessert. You also attempting it will not increase the likelihood of finishing the dessert and will likely only worsen things by getting in Martha's way.

11. In this second case, the thinking for yourself happened before getting the opinion of the relevant expert. This is just to show that the order that the relevant evidence is received is not relevant to what it is rational to believe. Whether the self-check is done before or after hearing the expert's diagnosis, it is rational to go with the expert.

12. In Lackey (2021b), the problem of predatory experts is raised for pre-emptive views of epistemic authority, like Zagzebski's. Zagzebski (2012 and 2013) has defended an influential account of epistemic authority according to which recognizing somebody as an epistemic authority provides you with preemptive reasons to take on their belief. As Zagzebski (2012) puts it, "[t]he fact that the authority has a belief p is a reason for me to believe p that replaces my other reasons relevant to believing p and is not simply added to them." (107) So, on the preemption view, you do not believe p on the basis of your own reasons, rather, it is entirely on the basis of the authority's reasons. Preemptive views of epistemic authority have also been discussed and defended by Keren (2007, 2014) and Constantin and Grundmann (2018). In contrast, total evidence views claim that expert testimony, while powerful evidence, is simply another piece of evidence to be added to your total evidence. As Lackey (2018) puts it, "the testimony of experts should always be regarded as a piece of evidence to be weighed with the other relevant evidence we have on the matter." (239) Such a view is also defended by Dormandy (2018) and Jager (2016).

13. For other calls for institutional solutions to epistemic problems, see Buzzell and Rini (2022), Goldman (2011), Rini (2017), and DiPaolo (forthcoming-a).

14. See also DiPaolo (forthcoming-b).

15. See also Abramson (2014: 16).

16. The same point can be made in the much more lighthearted case of a surprise party. Surprise parties work because the target of the surprise is being rational. They follow their reasons about what is, or is not, happening that night, and because of this, they can be surprised. While surprise parties have a 'gotcha!' moment, it is not due to any irrationality on the part of the surprised individual.

17. A somewhat related problematic case is deference in morally troubling communities. See Brinkman (2022) and Lackey (2018). For instance, consider a patriarchal community where wives are expected to adopt

their husband's political views. While there is plenty to be disturbed about regarding this society, it does not seem that it is the deference that is the problem. Rather, it is the social convention itself that is problematic. Brinkman (2022) also makes this point. See also Matheson (2016, 2021a) for discussion of a similar worry.

18. See also Levy (2022a), Noveck (2015), and Watson (2021).

8

1. This follows Elgin (2007) and Croce (2017).
2. See Kvanvig (2003), de Regt (2009), Pritchard (2009), Grimm (2010), and Gardiner (2012) for discussions of the epistemic value of understanding. See Grimm (2012) and Gordon (2022) for helpful overviews.
3. For more on the connection between curiosity and understanding, see Kvanvig (2003).
4. For more on this point, see Woodward (2003: 7).
5. Nickel (2001), Zagzebski (2007, 2012: 175–6), Hills (2009, 2013), Roberts and Wood (2010), Hazlett (2016), and Nguyen (2018b) are some examples.
6. The answer is c) I am Theresa's daughter.
7. Grimm (2006) maintains that knowledge is sufficient for understanding. This would be enough to block the understanding objection.
8. See Grimm (2011).
9. Another worry in the neighborhood concerns whether understanding why something is the case differs from knowing why it is the case. See Howell (2014: 397). While Hills insists that understanding why comes with a certain kind of know-how, it is not clear that knowing why cannot do so as well. Howell argues that even if we grant that know-how and know-that are distinct types of states, some knowledge might be such that it simply comes with know-how.
10. Recall the argument from evidential swamping in Chapter 3.
11. We might quibble with the 20% number, but wherever you set the number for what morality requires, it will still be true that you could have done even more and thereby brought about an even better state of affairs. For our purposes, that's all that we need to show. That you aren't required to bring about the best outcome.

12. For more on the concept of epistemically supererogatory acts, and the parallels to morally supererogatory acts, see Hedberg (2014) and Li (2018). See also Brinkman (2022) for an endorsement of the satisficing view (though he is thinking of things in moral terms).

13. Hedberg credits Tidman (1996) for inspiring this example.

14. This example also parallels one from Hedberg (2014). Yet another example given by Hedberg is an individual who dedicates an hour each night to reading an encyclopedia as opposed to relaxing by watching reruns of her favorite TV show. In doing so, she greatly adds to her number of true beliefs. While doing so, she improves her intellectual situation, she is going above and beyond the intellectual call of duty. There isn't an intellectual requirement to improve in these ways.

15. See Kappel (2010), Kelp (2014, 2020), Millar (2011), Rysiew (2012), Schaffer (2005), Whitcomb (2010, 2017), Williamson (2000). In addition to its relation to inquiry, knowledge has been seen as the norm of belief (Williamson 2000), the norm of action (Fantl and McGrath 2002, Hawthorne 2004, and Stanley 2005), and the norm of assertion (Benton 2011, Hawthorne 2004, Williamson 2000). See Benton (2022) for a summary of knowledge norms in epistemology.

16. See Millar (2011: 70).

17. For instance, see Hannon (2019) and Kelp (2014). Some philosophers have rejected that knowledge is the goal of inquiry, but in ways that are also compatible with our central conclusion. So long as the goal of inquiry is something that can be satisfied by deference, then doing more to gain understanding will be unnecessary. For instance, some have argued that the goal of inquiry is mere true belief. See Kvanvig (2003) and Lynch (2005). Others have seen the goal of inquiry as a rational belief. See Feldman (2002). Recently Falbo (2022) has argued that epistemic improvement is the aim of inquiry. Falbo is concerned with cases of legitimate inquiry where knowledge is not on the table. Falbo also wants to defend the claim that inquiring after one already knows is permissible. Of course, this too is compatible with the defense offered here.

18. Pritchard (2010) argues that understanding, rather than knowledge, is the goal of inquiry. If Pritchard is correct, then there would be a problem for our central conclusion. What motivates Pritchard's conclusion are cases where the subject has curiosity that extends beyond knowing

the answer – they also want to understand the answer. Remember, however, that it is consistent with our central conclusion that one wants more, epistemically speaking. All that is at issue here is whether it is *permissible* to stop at knowledge, and Pritchard's cases fail to tell against this. See Hannon (2019) for a further response to Pritchard.

9

1. Although, remember the caution about intellectual independence from Chapter 4. We are all intellectually dependent creatures.
2. See also King (2014).
3. See also Church and Barrett (2016) and Roberts and Wood (2010).
4. One worry here concerns how one could come to be aware of their intellectual limitations. Doesn't one have to think for themselves to discover their limitations? There are a couple things to be said here. First, recall that our central conclusion does not claim that thinking for yourself is never called for. Sometimes you are in the best, or a good enough, position to determine the answer. Second, it seems as though one legitimate way to discover your intellectual limitations is to learn about them from others. That is, it looks like you could defer to others about your limitations. For instance, you could come to believe that your evidential basis is insufficient by someone with a better evidential basis telling you so.
5. See also Watson (2019) and Whitcomb (2010).
6. One might object that curious individuals don't simply want knowledge; they also want understanding. It may be that virtuously curious people often want understanding, but what would be relevant to our point is whether desiring understanding is requisite for having the virtue of curiosity. It seems that one can be virtuously curious even if they are satisfied with simply knowing the answer.
7. See also King (2021) and Riggs (2010). On Riggs' account, open-mindedness is more inwardly focused, but still in a way that fits with our central conclusion. Much of what Riggs claims about open-mindedness is similar to the account of intellectual humility discussed earlier. On Riggs' account, "To be open-minded is to be aware of one's fallibility as a believer, and to be willing to acknowledge the possibility that anytime one believes something, it is possible that one is wrong." (180)

8. For instance, see Alfano, De Ridder, and Klein (2022), Byerly (2021), Croce (2017), Fricker (2007), Green (2016), and Kawall (2002). Though not coming from a virtue perspective, see also Grasswick (2020) and Lackey (2021a).

9. Green (2016) uses the analogy of team sports and team achievements.

10. Levy (2022c) comes to a similar conclusion though he is skeptical that there is much, if any, room for the intellectual virtues for individuals. As he puts it, "It is only in the narrow sphere of our own specialist expertise and our private lives that we ought to display the virtues. And this is the case because it is only in these spheres that we ought to be thinking for ourselves. For the rest, we ought to be deferring." (127).

11. On Croce's view, expertise requires the first set of virtues, while being an epistemic authority requires both. (2017: 494).

12. See also Grasswick (2020), Elgin (2002), and McCraw (2015, 2019) on appropriate trust relations, Roberts and Wood (2010) on testimonial credulity, and Notess (2019) on the virtue of listening.

13. The 'Straw Man Fallacy' is an informal fallacy where one mischaracterizes an individual's position or argument in a way that makes it easier to attack or refute.

14. See Goldberg (2011) and Worsnip (2019).

15. While Fricker was only concerned with credibility deficits, other philosophers have noted that similar problems of epistemic injustice emerge when individuals are given a credibility excess as well. See Lackey (2021a) and Medina (2012).

16. See also Fricker (2012).

17. This is not to say that individual virtues are sufficient to counteract epistemic injustice. It is plausible that institutional virtues are also needed. See Anderson (2012).

18. There are additional ways in which virtue epistemology can be socially enhanced. We have been focused on character virtues, but other virtue epistemologists focus on intellectual faculties and their reliability. For instance, Ahlstrom-Vij (forthcoming) is working with a consequentialist account of intellectual virtues, so on his account, for instance, having the proper motivation is not relevant to possessing a virtue. Ahlstrom-Vij makes an account for the virtue of deference, where this virtue is possessed "to the extent that one is disposed to listen to and believe those, and only those, speaking the truth." (214) In addition,

Ahlstrom-Vij posits a virtue of lending an ear, which is manifested to the extent that an individual is "disposed not only to speak the truth but also to listen in a way that promotes compliance and thereby also deference." (216) So, the virtue of lending an ear is a virtue possessed by the speaker which complements the virtue of deference, possessed by the hearer.

References and Further Reading

Aad, G. et al. (2015). (ATLAS Collaboration, CMS Collaboration). *Phys. Rev. Lett.* 114, 191803.

Abramson, K. (2014). "Turning up the lights on gaslighting." *Philosophical Perspectives* 28: 1–30.

Adamson, P. (2022). *Don't Think for Yourself: Authority and Belief in Medieval Philosophy.* University of Notre Dame Press.

Ahlstrom-Vij, K. (2013). *Epistemic Paternalism: A Defence.* Palgrave.

Ahlstrom-Vij, K. (2019). "The Epistemic Benefits of Democracy: A Critical Reflection." In M. Fricker, P. Graham, D. Henderson, N. Pederson, and J. Wyatt (eds.) *The Routledge Handbook of Social Epistemology.* New York: Routledge, 406–14.

Ahlstrom-Vij, K. (forthcoming). "The Epistemic Virtue of Deference." In H. Battaly (ed.), *The Routledge Handbook of Virtue Epistemology.* New York: Routledge, 276–96.

Alfano, M., De Ridder, J., and Klein, C. (eds.) (2022). D. New York: Routledge.

Anderson, E. (1995). "Knowledge, Human Interests, and Objectivity in Feminist Epistemology." *Philosophical Topics* 23(2): 27–58.

Anderson, E. (2006). "The Epistemology of Democracy." *Episteme: A Journal of Social Epistemology* 3(1): 8–22.

Anderson, E. (2011). "Democracy, Public Policy, and Lay Assessment of Scientific Testimony". *Episteme* 8: 144–164.

Anderson, E. (2012). "Epistemic Justice as a Virtue of Social Institutions." *Social Epistemology* 26(2): 163–73.

Antony, L. (1995). "Sisters, Please, I'd Rather do it Myself." *Philosophical Topics* 23: 59–94.

Aristotle (1991). *The Metaphysics.* Translated by John H. McMahon. Promethius.

Baehr, J. (2011). *The Inquiring Mind: On Intellectual Virtues and Virtue Epistemology*. Oxford: Oxford University Press.

Baier, A. (1985) *Postures of the Mind: Essays on Mind and Morals*. Minneapolis, MN: University of Minnesota Press.

Baier, A. 1986. "Trust and anti-trust." *Ethics* 96(2): 231–260.

Ballantyne, N. (2018). "Epistemic Tresspassing." *Mind* 128(510): 367–95.

Ballantyne, N. (2019). *Knowing our Limits*. Oxford University Press.

Ballantyne, N. (2022). "Novices and Expert Disagreement." In D. Dunning and N. Ballantyne (eds.) *Reason, Bias, and Inquiry*. New York: Oxford University Press, 227–253.

Ballantyne, N., & Dunning, D. (2022, January 3). Skeptics say, 'Do Your Own Research'. It's not that simple. *New York Times*. https://www.nytimes.com/2022/01/03/opinion/dyor-do-your-own-research.html

Battaly, H. (2016a). "Epistemic virtue and vice: Reliabilism, responsibilism, and personalism." In C. Mi, M. Slote, & E. Sosa (Eds.), *Moral and intellectual virtues in Western and Chinese philosophy* (pp. 99– 120). New York: Routledge.

Battaly, H. (2016b). "Developing virtue and rehabilitating vice: Worries about self-cultivation and self-reform." *Journal of Moral Education*, 45, 207–222. https://doi.org/10.1080/03057240.2016.1195732

Battaly, H. (2017). "Intellectual perseverance." *Journal of Moral Philosophy* 14: 669–697.

Battaly, H. (2021). "Intellectual Autonomy and Intellectual Interdependence." In J. Matheson and K. Lougheed (eds.), *Epistemic Autonomy*. Routledge. 153–172.

Battaly, H. and Slote, M. (2015). "Virtue epistemology and virtue ethics." In L. Besser-Jones and M. Slote (eds.), *The Routledge companion to virtue ethics*, New York: Routledge, pp. 253–269.

Benton, M. (2011). "Two More for the Knowledge Account of Assertion." *Analysis* 71: 684–687.

Benton, M. (2016). "Expert Opinion and Second-Hand Knowledge." *Philosophy and Phenomenological Research* 92: 492–508.

Benton, M. (2022). "Knowledge Norms." *The Internet Encyclopedia of Philosophy*. https://iep.utm.edu/kn-norms/ (accessed 6/01/2022).

Bird, A. (2010). Social knowing: The social sense of "scientific knowledge". *Philosophical Perspectives* 24: 23–56.

Bird, A. (2014). When is there a group that knows? Distributed cognition, scientific knowledge, and the social epistemic subject. In J. Lackey (Ed.), *Essays in Collective Epistemology* (pp. 42–63). Oxford University Press.

Bishop, M. A. (2005). "The Autonomy of Social Epistemology." *Episteme* 2:65–78.

Boyd, K. (2017). "Testifying Understanding." *Episteme* 14(1), 103–127.

Bokros, S. (2020). "A Deference Model of Epistemic Authority." *Synthese*

Brennan, J. (2014). "How Smart is Democracy? You Can't Answer That Question a Priori." *Critical Review* 26(1-2): 33–58.

Brighouse, H. (2005). *On education*. London: Routledge.

Brinkman, M. (2022). "In Defence of Non-Ideal Political Deference." *Episteme* 19(2): 264–85.

Budd, M. (2003). "The acquaintance principle." *The British Journal of Aesthetics* 43 (4):386–392.

Buzzell, A. and Rini, R. (2022). "Doing you own research and other impossible acts of epistemic superheroism." *Philosophical Psychology* https://doi.org/10.1080/09515089.2022.2138019

Byerly, R. (2021). *Intellectual Dependability: A Virtue Theory of the Epistemic and Educational Ideal*. New York: Routledge.

Byerly, R. and M. Byerly (2016). "Collective Virtue." *Journal of Value Inquiry* 50: 33–50.

Callahan, L.F. (2022). "Disagreement, Testimony, and Religious Understanding." *Religious Disagreement & Pluralism*. Edited by M. Benton and J. Kvanvig. Oxford: Oxford University Press, 41–64.

Carey, B. and Matheson, J. "How Skeptical is the Equal Weight View?" In D. Machuca (ed.) *Disagreement and Skepticism*, New York: Routledge, (2013) 131–49.

Carter, J.A. and Broncano-Berrocal, F. (2019) *The philosophy of group polarization: a collective vice theory*. Routledge. (Accepted for Publication)

Cassam, Q. 2018. *Vices of the Mind: From the Intellectual to the Political*. Oxford: Oxford University Press.

Cholbi, M. (2007). 'Moral Expertise and the Credentials Problem.' *Ethical Theory and Moral Practice* 10(4), 323–334.

Christensen, D. (2007). "The Epistemology of Disagreement: The Good News." *Philosophical Review* 116:187–218.

Christensen, D. (2010). "Higher-Order Evidence." *Philosophy and Phenomenological Research* 81(1): 185–215.

Christman, J. "Autonomy in Moral and Political Philosophy", The Stanford Encyclopedia of Philosophy (Fall 2020 Edition), E. N. Zalta (ed.), URL https://plato.stanford.edu/archives/fall2020/entries/autonomy-moral/

Church, I.M. and J. Barrett (2016). "Intellectual Humility." In E. L. Worthington Jr, D. E. Davis & J. N. Hook (eds.), *Routledge Handbook of Humility*. Springer.

Coady, C.A.J. (2002). "Testimony and intellectual autonomy." *Studies in History and Philosophy of Science Part A* 33(2): 355–372.

Code, L. (1991). *What can she know?: Feminist theory and the construction of knowledge*. Ithaca, NY: Cornell University Press.

Code, L. (2006). *Ecological Thinking: The Politics of Epistemic Location*. Oxford: Oxford University Press.

Constantin, J., and Grundmann, T. (2018). "Epistemic authority: Preemption through source sensitive defeat." *Synthese*. https://doi.org/10.1007/s11229-018-01923-x

Contessa, G. (2022). "Shopping for Experts." *Synthese* 200(3): 1–21.

Cook, J., Oreskes, N., Doran, P.T., Anderegg, W.R.L., Verheggen, B., Maibach, E.W., Carlton, J.S., Lewandowsky, S., Skuce, A.G. and Green, S.A. (2016). "Consensus on Consensus: A Synthesis of Consensus Estimates on Human-Caused Global Warming." *Environmental Research Letters* 11(4), Article 048002.

Craig, E. (1990) *Knowledge and the State of Nature*. Oxford: Clarendon Press.

Crisp, R. (2014). "Moral testimony pessimism: A defence." *Aristotelian Society Supplementary*, 88(1), 129–143. https://doi.org/10.1111/j.1467-8349.2014.00236.x

Croce, M. (2017). "Expert-oriented abilities vs. novice-oriented abilities: An alternative account of epistemic authority." *Episteme*. https://doi.org/10.1017/epi.2017.16

Croce, M. (2019). "On what it takes to be an expert." *The Philosophical Quarterly* 69(274), 1–21.

Dellsén, F. (2020). 'The Epistemic Value of Expert Autonomy.' *Philosophy and Phenomenological Research* 100(2), 344–61.

Dellsén, F. (2021). 'We Owe it to Others to Think for Ourselves.' In J. Matheson and K. Lougheed (eds), *Epistemic Autonomy*, pp. 306–22. New York, NY: Routledge.

Descartes, R. (1985/1628). "Rules for the Direction of the Mind." In Cottingham, J., Stoothoff, R., and Murdoch, D., editors, *The Philosophical Writings of Descartes*, volume I. Cambridge University Press, Cambridge.

de Regt, H.W. (2009). 'The Epistemic Value of Understanding.' *Philosophy of Science* 76(5), 585–97.

De Ridder, J. (2014). Epistemic dependence and collective scientific knowledge. *Synthese* 191(1), 37–53.

de Ridder, J. (2021). "Deep Disagreements and Political Polarization." In E. Edenberg and M. Hannon (eds.) *Political Epistemology*. New York: Oxford University Press, 226–243.

DiPaolo, J. (2022). "What's Wrong with Epistemic Trespassing?" *Philosophical Studies* 179: 223–43.

DiPaolo, J. (forthcoming-a). "I'm, Like, a Very Smart Person: On Self-Licensing and the Perils of Reflection." *Oxford Studies in Epistemology*. New York: Oxford University Press.

DiPaolo, J. (forthcoming-b) "Who Knows What? Epistemic Dependence, Inquiry, and Function-First Epistemology." *Inquiry*.

Dogramaci, S. (2012) "Reverse Engineering Epistemic Concepts." *Philosophy and Phenomenological Research* 84(3): 513–30.

Dormandy, K. (2018) "Epistemic Authority: Preemption or Proper Basing?" *Erkenntnis* 83(4): 773–791.

Driver, J. (2006). "Autonomy and the asymmetry problem for moral expertise." *Philosophical Studies: An International Journal for Philosophy in the Analytic Tradition* 128 (3): 619–644.

Dunning, D. (2005). *Self-Insight. Roadblocks and Detours on the Path to Knowing Thyself*. New York/Hove: Taylor and Francis.

Dunning, D. (2011). "The Dunning-Kruger Effect: On Being Ignorant of One's Own Ignorance." In J. Olson and M. Zanna (eds.) *Advances in Experimental Social Psychology*. San Diego, CA: Academic Press.

Dunning, D. (2022). "The Trouble of Not Knowing What You Do Not Know." In D. Dunning and N. Ballantyne (eds.) *Reason, Bias, and Inquiry*. New York: Oxford University Press. 205–226.

Ebels-Duggan, K. (2014). "Autonomy as Intellectual Virtue." In *The Aims of Higher Education*, Harry Brighouse and Michael MacPherson, eds. University of Chicago Press.

Elga, A. (2007). "Reflection and Disagreement." *Nous* 41:478–502.

Elgin, C. (2002) 'Take It from Me: The Epistemological Status of Testimony.' *Philosophy and Phenomenological Research* 65, pp. 291–308.

Elgin, C.Z. (2007). 'Understanding and the Facts.' *Philosophical Studies* 132: 33–42.

Elgin, C.Z. (2013) "Epistemic Agency," *Theory and Research in Education* 11(2): 135–152.

Elgin, C.Z. (2015) 'The Commonwealth of Epistemic Ends,' *The Ethics of Belief*, eds. Jonathan Matheson and Rico Vitz. Oxford: Oxford University Press, 2014, 244–260.

Elgin, C.Z. (2021) "The Realm of Epistemic Ends," In J. Matheson and K. Lougheed (eds.) *Epistemic Autonomy*. New York: Routledge.

Elster, J. and Landemore, H. (eds) (2012). *Collective Wisdom: Principles and Mechanisms*. Cambridge: Cambridge University Press.

Elzinga, B. (2019) "A relational account of intellectual autonomy." *Canadian Journal of Philosophy* 49(1): 22–47.

Encabo, J.V. (2008). 'Epistemic Merit, Autonomy, and Testimony.' *Theoria: An International Journal for Theory, History and Foundations of Science* 23(61), 45–56.

Estlund, D.M. (1994). "Opinion Leaders, Independence, and Condorcet's Jury Theorem". *Theory and Decision* 36: 131–162.

Falbo, A. (2022). "Inquiring Minds want to Improve." *Australasian Journal of Philosophy*. https://doi.org/10.1080/00048402.2021.2024863

Fantl, J. and M. McGrath (2002). "Evidence, Pragmatics, and Justification." *Philosophical Review* 111: 67–94.

Feinberg, J. (ed.) (1996). *Reason and Responsibility: Readings in Some Basic Problems of Philosophy*. 9th ed. Belmont, Calif.: Wadsworth.

Feldman, R. (2002). "Epistemological Duties." In Moser, P., editor, *The Oxford Handbook of Epistemology*. Oxford University Press, New York.

Feldman, R. (2006). "Reasonable Religious Disagreements." In Antony, L. M., editor, *Philosophers Without Gods: Meditations on Atheism and the Secular Life*, pages 194–214. Oxford University Press, Oxford.

Feldman, R. (2014). "Evidence of Evidence is Evidence." In Matheson, J. and Vitz, R. (eds.) *The Ethics of Belief: Individual and Social*. Oxford: Oxford University Press, 284–99.

Foley, R. (2001). *Intellectual Trust in Oneself and Others*. Cambridge University Press, Cambridge.

Foley, R. 1994. "Egoism in Epistemology", in *Socializing Epistemology: The Social Dimensions of Knowledge*, ed. F. Schmitt, Lanham, MD: Rowman & Littlefield: 53–73.

Frances, B. and J. Matheson, "Disagreement", *The Stanford Encyclopedia of Philosophy* (Winter 2019 Edition), Edward N. Zalta (ed.), URL = https://plato.stanford.edu/archives/win2019/entries/disagreement/

Fricker, E. (2006a). "Testimony and Epistemic Autonomy." In Lackey, J. and Sosa, E., editors, *The Epistemology of Testimony*, pages 225–251. Oxford University Press, Oxford.

Fricker, E. 2006b. "Second-Hand Knowledge." *Philosophy and Phenomenological Research* 73/3: 592–618.

Fricker, M. (2007). *Epistemic Injustice: Power and the Ethics of Knowing*. Oxford and New York: Oxford University Press.

Fricker, M. (2012). "Replies to Alcoff, Goldberg, and Hookway on *Epistemic Injustice*." *Episteme* 7(2): 164–78.

Fuerstein, M. (2013). 'Epistemic Trust and Liberal Justification.' *Journal of Political Philosophy* 21, 179–99.

Fumerton, R. (2010). 'You Can't Trust a Philosopher.' In R. Feldman and T. Warfield (eds), *Disagreement*, pp. 91–110. New York, NY: Oxford University Press.

Gardiner, G. (2012). 'Understanding, Integration, and Epistemic Value.' *Acta Analytica* 27(2), 163–81.

Gardiner, G. (2022). "Attunement: On the Cognitive Virtues of Attention." In M. Alfano, C. Klein, and J. De Ridder (eds.) *Social Virtue Epistemology*. New York: Routledge, 48–72.

Gerken, M. (2018). "Expert Trespassing Testimony and the Ethics of Science Communication." *Journal for General Philosophy of Science* 49 (3): 299–318.

Gerken, M. (2022) *Scientific Testimony: Its roles in science and society*. Oxford University Press.

Goldberg, S. 2010. *Relying on Others: An Essay in Epistemology*, Oxford: Oxford University Press.

Goldberg, Sanford. 2011. "If that were true I would have heard about it by now." In *The Oxford Handbook of Social Epistemology*. Oxford: Oxford University Press.

Goldberg, S. (2013). "Epistemic Dependence in Testimonial Belief, in the Classroom and Beyond," *Journal of Philosophy of Education* 47(2): 168–186.

Goldberg, S. (2022). "Expectations of Expertise: Boot-strapping in Social Epistemology." In M. Alfano, C. Klein, and J. De Ridder (eds.) *Social Virtue Epistemology*. New York: Routledge, 201–22.

Goldman, A. "Epistemic Paternalism: Communication Control in Law and Society." *Journal of Philosophy* 88, no. 3 (1991):113–31.

Goldman, A. (1999). *Knowledge in a Social World*. Oxford: Oxford University Press.

Goldman, A. (2001). "Experts: Which Ones Should You Trust?" *Philosophy and Phenomenological Research* 63:85–110.

Goldman, A. (2011). "A Guide to Social Epistemology", in Goldman and Whitcomb (eds.) *Social Epistemology: Essential Readings*, 11–37.

Goldman, A. (2016). Expertise. Topoi. https://doi.org/10.1007/s11245-016-9410-3

González de Prado, J. (2021). "Gaslighting, Humility, and the Manipulation of Rational Autonomy", in J. Matheson and K. Lougheed (eds.) *Epistemic Autonomy*. New York: Routledge.

Goodin, R. and List, C. (2001). "Epistemic Democracy: Generalizing the Condorcet Jury Theorem." *Journal of Political Philosophy* 9(3): 277–306.

Gordon, E. 2017. 'Social Epistemology and the Acquisition of Understanding.' In S. Grimm, C. Baumberger and S. Ammon (eds), *Explaining Understanding: New Perspectives from Epistemology and the Philosophy of Science*, pp. 293–317. New York, NY: Routledge.

Gordon, E. (2022). "Understanding in Epistemology." *The Internet Encyclopedia of Philosophy*: https://iep.utm.edu/understa/#H5 (accessed 5/24/2022).

Grasswick, H. (2018). "Epistemic Autonomy in a Social World of Knowing." In *The Routledge Handbook of Virtue Epistemology*, ed. H. Battaly. Routledge, 196–208.

Grasswick, H. 2020. "Reconciling Epistemic Trust and Responsibility." In *Trust in Epistemology*, edited by K. Dormandy, 161–188. New York: Routledge.

Green, A. (2016). *The Social Contexts of Intellectual Virtue: Knowledge as a Team Achievement*. New York: Routledge.

Grimm, S. (2006). Is understanding a species of knowledge? *British Journal for the Philosophy of Science* 57 (3):515–535.

Grimm, S. (2010). 'The Goal of Understanding.' *Studies in the History and Philosophy of Science* 41(4), 337–44.

Grimm, S. "Understanding" In S. Bernecker and D. Pritchard (eds.), *The Routledge Companion to Epistemology*. New York: Routledge, 2011.

Grimm, S. (2012). "The Value of Understanding." *Philosophy Compass* 7(2): 103–17.

Grundmann, T. (2021). 'Facing Epistemic Authorities: Where Democratic Ideals and Critical Thinking Mislead Cognition.' In S. Bernecker, A. Floweree and T. Grundmann (eds), *The Epistemology of Fake News*, pp. 134–55. Oxford: Oxford University Press.

Grundmann, T. (forthcoming). "Experts: What they are and how laypeople can identify them." In J. Lackey and A. McGlynn (eds.) *Oxford Handbook of Social Epistemology*. New York: Oxford University Press.

Guerrero, A. (2016). "Living with Ignorance in a World of Experts." In *Perspectives on Ignorance from Moral and Social Philosophy*, edited by R. Peels, 156–85. New York, NY: Routledge.

Why It's OK Not to Think for Yourself

Hannon, M. (2019) *What's the Point of Knowledge?* Oxford: Oxford University Press.

Hannon, M. (2022). "Is There a Duty to Speak Your Mind?" *Social Epistemology* https://doi.org/10.1080/02691728.2022.2045382

Hardwig, J. (1985). "Epistemic Dependence." *The Journal of Philosophy* 82:335–349.

Hardwig, J. (1991). "The Role of Trust in Knowledge." *The Journal of Philosophy* 88:693–708.

Hawthorne, J. (2004). *Knowledge and Lotteries*. Oxford: Oxford University Press.

Hazlett, A. (2016). "The Social Value of Non-Deferential Belief." *Australasian Journal of Philosophy* 94:131–151.

Hazlett, A. (2017). "Towards social accounts of testimonial asymmetries." *Noûs*, 51(1), 49–73.

Hedberg, T. (2014). "Epistemic supererogation and its implications." *Synthese* 191 (15):3621–3637.

Hills, A. (2009). "Moral testimony and moral epistemology." *Ethics*, 120(1), 94–127. https://doi.org/10.1086/648610

Hills, A. (2013). "Moral testimony." *Philosophy Compass*, 8(6), 552–559. https://doi.org/10.1111/phc3.12040

Hills, A. (2015). "Understanding why." *Noûs*, 49(2), 661–688.

Hinchman, L. (1996). "Autonomy, Individuality, and Self-Determination," in *What is Enlightenment? Eighteenth-Century Answers and Twentieth-Century Questions*, ed. J. Schmidt. Berkeley: University of California Press, 1996, 488–516.

Hopkins, R. (2007). "What is wrong with moral testimony?" *Philosophy and Phenomenological Research*, 74, 611–634. https://doi.org/10.1111/j.1933-1592.2007.00042.x

Hopkins, R. (2011). "How to be a skeptic about aesthetic testimony." *Journal of Philosophy*, 108(3), 138–157. https://doi.org/10.5840/jphil201110838

Howell, R. (2014). "Google Morals, Virtue, and the Asymmetry of Deference." *Noûs* 48(3): 389–415.

Huemer, M. (2005). "Is Critical Thinking Epistemically Responsible?" *Metaphilosophy* 36(4): 522–531.

Jaggar, A. (1983). *Feminist Politics and Human Nature*. Totowa, NJ: Rowman and Allanheld.

Jager, C. (2016) "Epistemic Authority, Preemptive Reasons, and Understanding." *Episteme* 13(2): 167–185.

Jensen, A., Joly Chock, V., Mallard, K., and Matheson, J. (2018). "Conscientiousness and other problems: A reply to Zagzebski." *Social Epistemology Review and Reply Collective* 7(1): 10–13.

Joly Chock, V. and Matheson, J. (2020). "Silencing, Epistemic Injustice, and Epistemic Paternalism." In *Epistemic Paternalism: Conceptions, Justifications, and Implications.* Eds. A. Bernal and G. Axtell. New York: Rowman & Littlefield. 219–232.

Jones, K. (1999). "Second-Hand moral knowledge." *Journal of Philosophy* 96 (2): 55–78.

Joshi, H. (2021). *Why It's OK to Speak Your Mind.* New York: Routledge.

Kahneman, D. (2011). *Thinking, fast and slow.* London & New York: Penguin Books.

Kant, I. (1991/1784). "An Answer to the Question: What is Enlightenment?" In Reiss, H., editor, *Political Writings*, pages 54–60. Cambridge University Press, Cambridge, 2nd edition.

Kant, I. (2005). *Critique of Judgement.* Trans. J. H. Bernard. New York: Dover, 2005.

Kappel, K. 2010. "On Saying That Someone Knows: Themes from Craig", in *Social Epistemology*, ed. A. Haddock, A. Millar, and D. Pritchard, Oxford: Oxford University Press: 69–88.

Kawall, J. (2002). "Other—Regarding Epistemic Virtues." *Ratio* 15(3):257–75.

Kelly, T. (2005). "The Epistemic Significance of Disagreement." In Gendler, T. and Hawthorne, J., editors, *Oxford Studies in Epistemology*, vol. 1, pages 167–196. Oxford University Press, Oxford.

Kelly, T. (2010). "Peer Disagreement and Higher Order Evidence." In Feldman, R. and Warfield, T., editors, *Disagreement*, pages 111–174. Oxford University Press, Oxford.

Kelly, T. (2011). "Consensus Gentium: Reflections on the 'Common Consent' Argument for the Existence of God", in *Evidence and Religious Belief* ed. K.J. Clark & R.J. VanArragon (Oxford, Oxford University Press): 135–156.

Kelp, C. (2011) "What's the Point of 'Knowledge' Anyway?" *Episteme* 8: 53–66.

Kelp, C. 2014. "Two for the Knowledge Goal of Inquiry." *American Philosophical Quarterly* 51/3: 227–32.

Kelp, C. (2018). "Inquiry, knowledge and understanding." *Synthese* 198 (Suppl 7):1583–1593

Kelp, C. 2020. "Theory of Inquiry." *Philosophy and Phenomenological Research* 103/2: 359–84.

Keren, A. (2007). "Epistemic authority, testimony, and the transmission of knowledge." *Episteme* 4(3): 368–381.

Keren, A. (2014). "Trust and belief: A preemptive reasons account." *Synthese* 191(12), 2593–2615.

King, N. (2014). "Perseverance as an Intellectual Virtue." *Synthese* 191: 3501–3523.

King, N. (2020). *The Excellent Mind: Intellectual Virtue for the Everyday Life.* Oxford University Press.

Kitcher, P. (1990). "The Division of Cognitive Labor." *Journal of Philosophy* 87:5–21.

Kitcher, P. (2001). *Science, Truth, and Democracy.* Oxford Studies in Philosophy of Science. New York: Oxford University Press.

Koppl, R. (2018). *Expert Failure.* Cambridge: Cambridge University Press.

Kornblith, H. (2010). "Belief in the Face of Controversy." In R. Feldman and F. Warfield (eds.) *Disagreement.* New York: Oxford University Press, 29–52.

Kvanvig, J. (2003). *The Value of Knowledge and the Pursuit of Understanding.* New York, NY: Cambridge University Press.

Kvanvig, J.L. 2009. "The Value of Understanding." In *Epistemic Value*, ed. A. Haddock, D. Pritchard, and A. Millar, Oxford: Oxford University Press: 95–111.

LaBarge, S. (1997). "Socrates and the recognition of experts." *Apeiron: A Journal for Ancient Philosophy and Science* 30 (4): 51–62.

Lackey, J. (2006). "Knowing from Testimony." *Philosophy Compass* 1(5): 432–448.

Lackey, J. (2010). "A Justificationalist View of Disagreement's Epistemic Significance." In Haddock, A., Millar, A., and Pritchard, D., editors, *Social Epistemology*, pages 298–325. Oxford University Press, Oxford.

Lackey, J. (2018). "Experts and peer disagreement." In M. A. Benton, J. Hawthorne, & D. Rabinowitz (Eds.), *Knowledge, belief, and god: New insights in religious epistemology* (pp. 228–245). Oxford: Oxford University Press.

Lackey, J. (2021a). "Epistemic Duties Regarding Others." In *Epistemic Duties: New Arguments, New Angles*, K. McCain and S. Stapleford (eds.). New York: Routledge, 281–295.

Lackey, J. (2021b). "Preemption and the Problem of Predatory Experts." *Philosophical Topics* 49(2): 133–150.

Laetz, B. "A Modest Defense of Aesthetic Testimony." *The Journal of Aesthetics and Art Criticism* 66.4 (2008): 355– 63.

Landemore, H. (2012). 'Democratic Reason: The Mechanisms of Collective Intelligence in Politics.' In Landemore, H. and Elster, J. (eds), *Collective Wisdom: Principles and Mechanisms*, pp. 251–89. Cambridge: Cambridge University Press.

Lane, M. (2014). 'When the Experts are Uncertain: Scientific Knowledge and the Ethics of Democratic Judgment.' *Episteme* 11, 97–118.

Levy, N. (2007). 'Radically Socialized Epistemology.' *Episteme* 4(2), 181–92.

Levy, N. (2021). *Bad Beliefs: Why They Happen to Good People*. Oxford: Oxford University Press.

Levy, N. (2022a). "Do Your Own Research!" *Synthese* 200(356). https://doi.org/10.1007/s11229-022-03793-w

Levy, N. (2022b). "In Trust We Trust: Epistemic Vigilance and Responsibility." *Social Epistemology* 36 (3):283–298.

Levy, N. (2022c). "Narrowing the Scope of Virtue Epistemology." In M. Alfano, C. Klien, and J. de Ridder (eds.) *Social Virtue Epistemology*. New York: Routledge, 113–30.

Li, H. (2018). "A Theory of Epistemic Supererogation." *Erkenntnis* 83 (2):349–367.

Lillehammer, H. (2014). 'Moral Testimony, Moral Virtue, and the Value of Autonomy.' *Aristotelian Society Supplementary Volume* 88, 111–27.

List, C. and P. Pettit (2004) "An Epistemic Free-Riding Problem" in *Karl Popper: Critical Appraisals*, ed. P. Catton and G. Macdonald, Abingdon: Routledge: 128–58.

List, C. and Goodin, R. (2001). "Epistemic Democracy: Generalizing the Condorcet Jury Theorem." *The Journal of Political Philosophy* 9(3): 277–306.

Locke, J. (1975/1689). *An Essay Concerning Human Understanding*. Clarendon Press, Oxford.

Lynch, M. (2005). *True To Life. Why Truth Matters*. MIT Press, Cambridge/MA.

Lynch, M. (2016). *The Internet of Us. Knowing More and Understanding Less in the Age of Big Data*. New York: Liveright Publishing.

Lynch, M. (2019). *Know-It-All Society. Truth and Arrogance in Political Culture*. New York & London: Liveright.

Mackenzie, C., and Stoljar, N. (eds.) (2000). *Relational Autonomy: Feminist Perspectives on Autonomy, Agency, and the Social Self*. Oxford: Oxford University Press.

McCraw, B. (2015). "The Nature of Epistemic Trust." *Social Epistemology* 29(4): 413–30.

McCraw, B. (2019). "Proper Epistemic Trust as a Responsibilist Virtue." In *Trust in Epistemology*, ed. K. Dormandy. Routledge, 189–217.

McGrath, S. (2008). "Moral disagreement and moral expertise." *Oxford Studies in Metaethics* 3:87–108.

McGrath, S. (2009). "The Puzzle of Pure Moral Deference." *Philosophical Perspectives* 23, no. 1: 321–344.

McGrath, S. 2011. "Skepticism about moral expertise as a puzzle for moral realism" *Journal of Philosophy*, 3. 111–137.

McMyler, B. (2011) *Testimony, Trust, and Authority*. Oxford: Oxford University Press.

Martini, C. (2014). Experts in science: a view from the trenches. *Synthese*, 191, pp. 3–15.

Martini, C. (2020). "The Epistemology of Expertise". In: M. Fricker, P. Graham, D. Henderson & N.J.L.L. Pedersen, *The Routledge Handbook of Social Epistemology*, London, New York: Routledge: 115–122.

Matheson, J. (2009). "Conciliatory Views of Disagreement and Higher-Order Evidence," *Episteme: A Journal of Social Philosophy* 6(3): 269–279.

Matheson, J. (2015). *The Epistemic Significance of Disagreement*. Palgrave Macmillan, Basingstoke.

Matheson, J. (2016). "Moral Caution and the Epistemology of Disagreement," *Journal of Social Philosophy* 47(2): 120–141.

Matheson, J. (2021a). "Applying Moral Caution in the Face of Disagreement," *Ethical Theory and Moral Practice*.

Matheson, J. (2021b). "The Argument from Common Consent." In *Contemporary Arguments in Natural Theology*. Ed. C. Ruloff. (2021) Bloomsbury Press.

Matheson, J. (2021c). "The Virtue of Epistemic Autonomy." In *Epistemic Autonomy*. Eds. Kirk Lougheed and Jonathan Matheson. Routledge.

Matheson, J. (2022). "Why Think for Yourself?" *Episteme*.

Matheson, J. (forthcoming). "Evidentialism & Social Epistemology." In *Oxford Handbook of Social Epistemology*. Eds. J. Lackey and A. McGlynn.

Matheson, J. and Lougheed, K. (eds.) (2021a). *Epistemic Autonomy*. New York: Routledge.

Matheson, J. and Lougheed, K. (2021b). "Introduction: Puzzles Concerning Epistemic Autonomy." In *Epistemic Autonomy*. Eds. K. Lougheed and J. Matheson. New York: Routledge.

Matheson, J., McElreath, S., and Nobis, N. (2018). "Moral Experts, Deference & Disagreement." In *Moral Expertise: New Essays from Theoretical and Clinical Perspectives*. Eds. J. Watson and L. Guidry-Grimes. Springer, (2018) 87–105.

Medina, J. (2012) *The Epistemology of Resistance*. New York: Oxford University Press.

Meskin, A. (2004) "Aesthetic Testimony: What Can We Learn From Others About Beauty and Art?" *Philosophy and Phenomenological Research* 69.1: 65–91.

Mill, J. S. *On Liberty*. Indianapolis and New York: The Liberal Arts Press, 1956; originally published 1859.

Millar, A. (2011). "Why Knowledge Matters." *Aristotelian Society Supp. Vol.* 85/1: 63–81.

Millgram, E. (2015). *The Great Endarkenment: Philosophy for An Age of Hyperspecialization*. Oxford: Oxford University Press.

Mogensen, A. L. (2015). "Moral Testimony Pessimism and the Uncertain Value of Authenticity." *Philosophy and Phenomenological Research* 92, no. 3: 1–24.

Nedelsky, J. (1989). 'Reconceiving Autonomy: Sources, Thoughts and Possibilities.' *Yale Journal of Law and Feminism* 1, 7–36.

Nehamas, A. (1998). *The Art of Living*. (Berkeley, CA: University of California Press).

Nguyen, C. T. (2010). "Autonomy, understanding, and moral disagreement." *Philosophical Topics* 38 (2): 111–129.

Nguyen, C. T. (2018a). "Cognitive islands and runaway echo chambers: problems for epistemic dependence on experts," in *Synthese*, https://doi.org/10.1007/s11229-018-1692-0

Nguyen, C.T. (2018b) "Expertise and the Fragmentation of Intellectual Autonomy" *Philosophical Inquiries* 6(2) 107–124

Nickel, P. (2001). 'Moral Testimony and its Authority.' *Ethical Theory and Moral Practice* 4(3), 253–66.

Nietzsche, F. (1966). *Beyond Good and Evil*. Translated by W. Kaufmann. New York: Random House.

Notess, S. (2019). "Listening to People: Using Social Psychology to Spotlight an Overlooked Virtue." *Philosophy* 94(4): 621–43.

Noveck, B.S. (2015). *Smart Citizens, Smarter State*. Harvard University Press.

Nussbaum, M. (2017). *Not for Profit:Why Democracy Needs the Humanities* (Updated Edition). Princeton University Press, Princeton.

Oreskes, N. (2019). *Why Trust Science?*, Princeton University Press.

Oshana, M. (2008). "Personal autonomy and society." *The Journal of Social Philosophy* 29(1): 81–102.

Palermos, S.O., & Pritchard, D. (2016). The distribution of epistemic agency. *Social epistemology and epistemic agency: De-centralizing epistemic agency* 109–26.

Palermos, S.O. (2020). "Epistemic collaborations: distributed cognition and virtue reliabilism." *Erkenntnis*. https://doi.org/10.1007/s10670-020-00258-9

Plato (1997). *Plato: Complete Works*. Edited by J. Cooper. Translated by G.M.A. Grube. Indianapolis, Indiana: Hackett Publishing Co.

Pettit, P. (2006) "When to Defer to Majority Testimony, and When not to." *Analysis* 66(3): DOI:10.1093/analys/66.3.179

Pojman, L. (ed.) (1991). *Introduction to Philosophy: Classical and Contemporary Readings*. Belmont, Calif.: Wadsworth.

Polanyi, M. and Prosch, H. (1977) *Meaning*. Chicago: Chicago University Press.

Pritchard, D. (2009). 'Knowledge, Understanding and Epistemic Value.' *Royal Institute of Philosophy Supplements* 64, 19–43.

Pritchard, D. (2016). 'Seeing It for Oneself: Perceptual Knowledge, Understanding, and Intellectual Autonomy.' *Episteme* 13(1), 29–42.

Pritchard, D., Millar, A., and Haddock, A. (2012). *The Nature and Value of Knowledge: Three Investigations*. (reprint edition). New York: Oxford University Press.

Pritchard, D. (2022). "Cultivating Intellectual Virtues." In R. Curren (ed.) *Routledge Handbook of Philosophy of Education*. New York: Routledge.

Ranalli, C. (2019). "The Puzzle of Philosophical Testimony" *European Journal of Philosophy* (2019) 1–22.

Raz, J. (1988). *The Morality of Freedom*. Oxford: Claredon Press.

Reid, T. (1827). *Essays on the Powers of the Human Mind*. London: Thomas Davidson, Whitefriars.

Reid, T. (1785/1983). *Essays on the Intellectual Powers of Man*. Excerpts reprinted in Beanblossom and Lehrer (eds.) Inquiry Essays and (Indianapolis, IN: Hackett): 127–284.

Rieder, G. and Simon, J. (2016). "Datatrust: Or, the Political Quest for Numerical Evidence and Epistemologies of Big Data." *Big Data and Society* 3(1): 1–6.

Riggs, W. (2010). "Open-Mindedness." *Metaphilosophy* 41: 172–88.

Rini, R. (2017). "Fake News and Partisan Epistemology." *Kennedy Institute of Ethics Journal* 27: 43–64.

Roberts, R.C. and W.J. Wood (2010). *Intellectual Virtues: An Essay in Regulative Epistemology*. New York: Oxford University Press.

Robertson, E. (2016). "Testimonial Virtue." In J. Baehr (ed.) *Intellectual Virtues and Education: Essays in Applied Virtue Epistemology*. New York: Routledge, 128–41.

Robson, J. (2012). Aesthetic testimony. *Philosophy Compass* 7(1): 1–10. https://doi.org/10.1111/j.1747-9991.2011.00455.x

Robson, J. (2013). "Aesthetic testimony and the norms of belief formation." *European Journal of Philosophy*, 23(3), 750–763.

Rowley, W. (2018). "An Evidentialist Social Epistemology." In K. McCain (ed.) *Believing According to the Evidence: New Essays on Evidentialism*. Springer, p. 127–43.

Ryan, S. (2021). "Autonomy, Reflection, and Education," In J. Matheson and K. Lougheed (eds.) *Epistemic Autonomy*. New York: Routledge.

Rysiew, P. 2012. "Epistemic Scorekeeping." in *Knowledge Ascriptions*, ed. J. Brown and M. Gerken, Oxford: Oxford University Press: 270–94.

Scanlon, T. (1972). "A Theory of Freedom of Expression," *Philosophy and Public Affairs*, i, 2: 204–26.

Schaffer, J. 2005. "Contrastive Knowledge." in *Oxford Studies in Epistemology*, Vol. 1, ed. T.S. Gendler and J. Hawthorne, Oxford: Clarendon Press: 235–71.

Schmitt, F. (1987). "Justification, Sociality, and Autonomy." *Synthese* 73: 43–85.

Schmitt, F.F. (2010). "The Assurance View of Testimony." In *Social Epistemology*, edited by A. Haddock, A. Millar, and D. Pritchard, 216–42. Oxford and New York: Oxford University Press.

Seigel, H. (1988). *Educating reason: Rationality, critical thinking, and education*. New York: Routledge.

Shafer-Landau, R. 1998. 'Ethical Subjectivism'. In *Reason and Responsibility: Readings in Some Basic Problems of Philosophy*, J. Feinberg and R. Shafer-Landau (eds). Wadsworth.

Shanteau, J. (1992). "The psychology of experts an alternative view." In: G. Wright and F. Bolger eds., *Expertise and Decision Support*, NY: Plenum Press, pp. 11–23.

Shanteau, J. (2000). 'Why do experts disagree?' In: Green, B., Cressy, R., Delmar, F., Eisenberg, T., Howcroft, B., Lewis, M., Schoenmaker, D., Shanteau, J., & Vivian, R. eds., *Risk behaviour and Risk Management in Business Life*. Dordrecht, The Netherlands: Kluwer Academic Press, pp. 186–196.

Shanteau, J. et al. (2002). Performance-based assessment of expertise: how to decide if someone is an expert or not. *European Journal of Operational Research*, 136(2), pp. 253–263.

Shieber, J. (2010) "Between Autonomy and Authority: Kant on the Epistemic Status of Testimony" *Philosophy and Phenomenological Research* 80(2): 327–48.

Skipper, M. (forthcoming). "Wise Groups and Humble Persons: The Best of Both Worlds?" *Asian Journal of Philosophy*.

Sibley, F. (1965). 'Aesthetic and Nonaesthetic', *The Philosophical Review* 74(2): 135–59.

Sliwa, P. (2012). "In defense of moral testimony." *Philosophical Studies* 158(2), 175–195. https://doi.org/10.1007/s11098-012-9887-6

Sliwa, P. (2015). "Understanding and knowing." *Proceedings of the Aristotelian Society*, 115(1pt1), 57–74. https://doi.org/10.1111/j.1467-9264.2015.00384.x

Smith, M. (1994). *The Moral Problem*. (Malden, MA: Blackwell).

Smith, M. (2000). "Moral Realism." Reprinted in his *Ethics and the A Priori* (Cambridge: Cambridge University Press, 2004).

Solomon, M. (2010). "Groupthink vs. the Wisdom of Crowds: The Social Epistemology of Deliberation and Dissent", *The Southern Journal of Philosophy* 44: 28–42.

Sosa, E. (2021). *Epistemic explanations: A theory of telic normativity, and what it explains*. Oxford University Press.

Spear, A. (2019) "Epistemic Dimensions of Gaslighting: Peer-Disagreement, Self-Trust, and Epistemic Injustice." *Inquiry*: 1–24.

Stanley, Jason. 2005. *Knowledge and Practical Interests*. Oxford: Oxford University Press.

Surowiecki, J. (2004). *The Wisdom of Crowds*. New York, NY: Doubleday.

Sunstein, Cass (2008). *Infotopia: How Many Minds Produce Knowledge*. Oxford: Oxford University Press.

Tanesini, A. (2021) *The Mismeasure of the Self. A Study in Vice Epistemology*. Oxford: Oxford University Press.

Tidman, P. (1996). "Critical reflection: an alleged epistemic duty." *Analysis* (56)4, 268–276

Tsai, G. (2014) "Rational Persuasion as Paternalism" *Philosophy and Public Affairs* 42(1): 78–112.

van Wietmarschen, H. (2018). 'Political Testimony.' *Politics, Philosophy & Economics* 18: 23–45

Watson, J. (2021). *Expertise: A Philosophical Introduction*. Bloomsbury Publishing.

Watson, L. (2019). "Curiosity and Inquisitiveness." In *The Routledge Handbook of Virtue Epistemology*. Ed. H. Battaly. New York: Routledge.

Westlund, A. (2012). 'Autonomy in Relation.' In S.L. Crasnow and A.M. Superson (eds), *Out from the Shadows: Analytical Feminist Contributions to Traditional Philosophy*, pp. 59–81. New York, NY: Oxford University Press.

Whitcomb, D. 2010. "Curiosity Was Framed." *Philosophy and Phenomenological Research* 81/3: 664–87.

Whitcomb, D. 2017. "One Kind of Asking." *The Philosophical Quarterly* 67/266: 148–68.

Whitcomb, D., Battaly, H., Baehr, J., & Howard-Snyder, D. (2017). "Intellectual humility: Owning our limitations." *Philosophy and Phenomenological Research*, **XCIV**, 509–539.

Whitcomb, D. et al. "The Puzzle of Humility and Disparity" Forthcoming in *Routledge Handbook of the Philosophy of Humility*, eds. Alfano, Lynch, and Tanesini.

Wolff, R.P. (1970). *In Defense of Anarchism*. London: Harper and Row.

Woodward, J. (2003). *Making Things Happen: A Theory of Causal Explanation*. New York: Oxford University Press.

Worsnip, A. (2019). "The Obligation to Diversify One's Sources: Against Epistemic Partisanship in the Consumption of News Media." In C. Fox & J. Saunders (eds.), *Media Ethics: Free Speech and the Requirements of Democracy*. London: Routledge. pp. 240–264.

Williamson, T. (2000). *Knowledge and its Limits*. New York: Oxford University Press.

Zagzebski, L. (2007). "Ethical and Epistemic Egoism and the Ideal of Autonomy." *Episteme* 4:252–263.

Zagzebski, L.T. (2011). "Epistemic Self-Trust and the Consensus Gentium Argument", in *Evidence and Belief Religious* ed. K.J. Clark and R.J. VanArragon (Oxford, Oxford University Press: 22–36.

Zagzebski, L.T. (2012). *Epistemic Authority: A Theory of Trust, Authority, and Autonomy in Belief*, New York: Oxford University Press.

Zagzebski, L.T. (2013). "Intellectual autonomy." *Philosophical Issues* 23: 244–261.

Zollman, K. (2012). "Network Epistemology: Communication in Epistemic Communities." *Philosophy Compass* 8: 15–27.

Index

Printed in the United States
by Baker & Taylor Publisher Services